1 0 1
SECRETS TO
NEGOTIATING
SUCCESS

BY ELAINE F. RÉ, PH.D.

Elaine F Ré

Canyon Crest Publishing
1721 Quail Run CT. NE
Albuquerque, NM 87122
1-800-724-3301
www.CanyonCrestPublishing.com

Library of Congress Catalogue Number: 98-073721
ISBN: 0-9666933-0-2

This publication is designed to provide accurate and authoritative information in regard to the subject matter conveyed. It is sold with the understanding that the publisher is not engaged in rendering legal, accounting, or other professional service. If legal advice or other expert assistance is required, the service of a competent professional person should be sought.

ACKNOWLEDGEMETS

This book would never have come into existence without the vision of my partner, publisher and friend, Astrid Lugowski, who took over the dream and turned it into a reality. To her I am most grateful.

I would also like to express my thanks to:

- Thomas Ré, whose foresight, guidance and tenacity caused me to be on this life path. He is always there to listen, to advise, and, most importantly, to care;

- The person who believed in and encouraged me all along my professional journey - Stacey Schilling;

- All the people who supported me and provided opportunities for me to learn, practice and perform at the American Management Association especially: Maddy Epstein, Jackie Green, Sandy Held, Andrea Iadanza and Ann O'Connor;

- Phyllis White, who, in 1978, challenged me to write my first course on Negotiation and who always said, "Of course you can," whenever doubt entered my mind;

I also owe much thanks to the hundreds of people who participated in my negotiation seminars, from whom I learned more than they can ever know. What a pleasure it has been to get to know them and to watch them turn my theories into successful practice. I have been rewarded many times by their phone calls and letters expressing excitement over negotiation successes they experienced.

A very special thank you goes to my canine companion of 14 years, Demitasse, the "Vice President of Security" who loyally lay in her chair by my desk continually waiting for me to "finish." (She was not alone!)

TABLE OF CONTENTS

Preparing For The Other Side

Putting Together The Plan

Plotting The Course

Personal Preparation

PART II: WHILE YOU ARE NEGOTIATING

And You're Off!

PART III: AFTER YOU NEGOTIATE

INTRODUCTION

Thisbook holds the secrets to successful negotiations.

Believe it or not, you already have the background you need to use this book: experience in the real world. As you will learn, your life is and always has been a daily series of negotiations, from the simplest decisions of everyday living to the most complicated issues you have to resolve. Negotiations are an inevitable and unavoidable part of your life. The key lies in knowing how to get through each negotiation quickly and easily, and coming out a winner every time. That's where this book will help you.

Based upon years of practical experience and decades of teaching business people how to negotiate, the secrets you are about to read are time-tested and guaranteed to turn you into a more effective negotiator. Helpful hints, useful tools, and successful techniques will all be at your disposal in each of three sections, covering the whole preparation process before you begin negotiations, strategies and tactics to use while you're negotiating, and what should happen after negotiations have ended.

There is no need to read this book from beginning to end (unless you want to). It has been designed to give you tips that you can start to use *right now* to improve your negotiating skills and to get just about everything you want out of every negotiation you enter into. So before beginning, look over the table of contents and pick out those topics of most immediate concern to you, and those issues that are most important to you in how you currently negotiate. Read those secrets first, and you'll find that the easy tips and practical suggestions in this book can be put to immediate use as you negotiate for both every-day things *and* big-ticket items.

This is not a boring business book about theory. It is a practical, hands-on tool for becoming a better negotiator *now*. I know you will enjoy the positive results you'll gain as you learn how to get what you need from other people. You can do it!

1 0 1
SECRETS TO
NEGOTIATING
S U C C E S S

PART I

BEFORE YOU NEGOTIATE

THE STUFF OF WHICH
SUCCESSFUL NEGOTIATIONS ARE MADE

Here are three hypothetical situations. Read them over, and decide which of these situations describe the beginning of a true negotiation:

- A little girl goes with her dad to a shopping center. Dad is the one, of course, with the money in his pocket—and his daughter knows this. "Hey, Daddy, can I have an ice cream cone?" Her father replies: "You want one now?" "Yes!" she urges him. "I won't tell Mom!"

- A man's boss calls him into the office and out of the blue says, "Joe, I'd like to offer you a raise." Joe looks around to see if there's anybody else with his name in the room. "You want to offer me a raise?" he asks skeptically.

- A prisoner in jail calls out to his jailer: "Hey! Give me a cigarette!" The jailer shakes his head. "You know the rules. No cigarettes." "Aw, come on," says the prisoner, "Give me a cigarette, willya?"

So which of these marks the beginning of a real negotiation? All of them, of course! And they all have something in common, too. In every single case, there is the potential for both sides of the equation to be gain-

DOUBLE EXCHANGE

In negotiations, both parties exchange something the other person values.

ing something positive. The little girl may win her ice cream cone, while her dad will earn the reward of a hug and a kiss and a delighted giggle. The worker may gain an unexpected but welcome increase in pay, undoubtedly as recognition of his accomplishments and abilities, while his boss will gain a more motivated employee in the bargain. The prisoner may get his cigarette, and in return his jailer may earn the respect and the cooperation from the man behind the bars.

For everything that is given, something is gained in return. And for every negotiation that is begun, the question that underlies it will always be: "What's in it for me?" That's something that all negotiations share, and supplies the foundation for almost every secret of successful negotiating, as you will see.

#1: It's a fact: You are always negotiating!

Yes, it's true. From the moment you get up in the morning, throughout your work day, and until you go to sleep at night, your day is filled with negotiating. You may not always realize it, but the fact is that you are continually engaging in a negotiating process of some kind or another.

Think about it for a moment. Consider all that you do in the course of a typical day, and you'll find that you encounter several negotiations as you go along. For instance: You have to agree with your spouse about which movie to see. Your teenager is begging you to let him use the family car. You must ask your boss for time off to take a vacation. You have a date, and are trying to come to a mutual decision on where to go for dinner. You're at dinner, and want to replace your potato with a salad. You have an important deadline, and require the cooperation of other key people if you're to meet it. You're driving on the highway and need to negotiate with other drivers to get from the far left lane into the far right if you're going to make your exit in time.

And on it goes. Each and every day, you are faced with situations that involve an exchange necessary to satisfy the needs of both parties. That's a negotiation.

Negotiation is not a new process. It's something you've been doing ever since you cried for food as a baby, and maybe even before you were born. In fact, believe it or not, you're already good at negotiating, if only because you've been doing it for so long! You even negotiate with yourself, with just about every decision you have to make, large or small. You are always having to identify a goal or need, weigh the alternatives, and arrive at an equitable solution. That's what you do in everyday life, and that's what negotiators do. Simple, isn't it?

So keep that in mind as you enter into any formal negotiation. Apply the same principles and tactics that you use (consciously or otherwise) in your ordinary, daily negotiations, and you'll be well on your way to winning even the most important negotiations of your life. Ultimately, you will find that you're a much better negotiator than you think!

#2: Every negotiation is a trade

The fact is, life is a series of trades, and negotiating is the means by which we bring about a successful trade, where both parties are satisfied with the end result.

In most trading relationships, each side of the party has something the other wants or needs. Thus, the ideal attitude in a negotiation, and the one more prevalent at professional levels, requires that both sides must become partners in arriving at a solution, rather than being adversaries or competitors. Whatever the outcome, the result must be mutually beneficial, and perceived as such by both parties.

Thus, every negotiation you enter into will be a trade. You will give something in order to get something in return. For a truly successful negotiation, you need to position your proposal in such a way that the other party clearly sees it is favorable to enter into an agreement with you. The trade must be mutually beneficial or it will never work. Remember this fact, because it will be the cornerstone of just about every negotiation you enter into!

WHAT NEGOTIATING IS

A negotiation is the process of:

✓ *seasoned cooperation between two parties*

✓ *both parties gaining from the agreement—mutually satisfying needs*

✓ *communicating back and forth to reach an agreement when you and the other side have some interests that are shared and others that are opposed*

✓ *accurately observing, realistically assuming, correctly analyzing, logically planning behavior, and optimally preparing for each moment of a changing bargaining situation*

✓ *focusing on gaining the favor of people from whom we want things*

✓ *trading something of value to the other party to receive something of value to us in return*

✓ *arriving at a mutually agreeable settlement*

#3: Every negotiation involves concessions— or the appearance of a compromise

A s the Rolling Stones song goes, "You can't always get what you want." That is just a fact of life. If everybody involved in a negotiation held out for only getting what they wanted, without giving anything in return, there would never be a satisfactory agreement. In order to get a little, we have to give a little. And that means being willing to make concessions.

Don't get me wrong. This doesn't mean giving away the store. But the chances are pretty good that there is going to have to be *something* that you need to give up in order to get what you really need out of the negotiation. And the chances are also pretty good that whatever you give up this time around may be gained back the next time because you have fostered a good business relationship by your willingness to make concessions in this particular negotiation—which in turn makes the other side more amenable and pliable for the next go-round.

You can prepare for the inevitability of concessions by making sure you have at least a couple of issues that aren't very important to you, so that you can trade them for something that is of value to you. Good planning will ensure that you don't have to compromise on those needs that matter the most, by being able to give up that which matters the least. After all, compromise usually involves giving "something" up. If that "something" is important in each person's case, then the result is that both people lose. This is what is called, " lose-lose." However, if the "something" you give up is only a deviation from your Maximum Supportable position, or is unimportant to you, then you've appeared to compromise and will have achieved a great settlement.

The best alternative is to create a larger whole that encompasses both people's real needs. Sometimes, however, your material needs will be just too far apart, and a mutually satisfactory agreement won't be possible, no matter how many compromises are made. In fact, if there are too many concessions, then nothing is truly gained for either side, and it is better just to give up and go home.

You will hear it said many times over in this book that a successful negotiation is a win-win situation. For concessions to work, they must create the effect that something has been gained, not lost. You should never give anything up without getting something in return. Only then will the art of making concessions work for you. (See #55-59.)

WHAT NEGOTIATING IS NOT

A negotiation is

✓ *not a confrontation*

✓ *not win-lose*

✓ *not getting all you can, no matter what*

✓ *not walking away with less, if there is more to get*

✓ *not a triumph of the powerful over the weak*

✓ *not a mudslinging contest*

✓ *not intimidation*

Remember: Every "No" is a definite "Maybe" !

#4: A demand, a request, or an offer

All negotiations begin with a demand, a request, or an offer. You can bet on it.

When one party demands attention to an issue, requests a favor, or offers a service to another party, how the other party responds to it will determine the negotiation process. If the answer is immediate agreement, then there is an immediate exchange. This is easiest for the party making the demand, request or offer, but could have the undesired effect of causing the other party to miss significant opportunities. If the answer is "maybe," then both parties can start to negotiate the specific issues involved. This outcome allows the most opportunity for a mutually satisfying agreement. But if the answer is an immediate refusal, the two parties reach what appears to be a deadlock. They will need to continue to probe each other's reasons and concerns to determine alternate solutions. If, after several attempts, the answer remains, "no," then a deadlock results. Without a mutually satisfactory agreement, any deal will fall through. If two parties truly want to work with each other, then they need to push past the impasse into a negotiating situation.

To reduce the negotiation process to its simplest

terms, every negotiation begins with a straightfor-
ward demand, request, or offer, and it proceeds as
a result of the other party's response. Whether or
not you are the initiator of the negotiation, your
goal should always be to aim for the "maybe" cat-
egory, since this allows for the greatest chance of
a win-win outcome.

#5: Successful negotiations should be win-win

There are two types of negotiation: Competitive negotiations that exist on a one-time-only basis (i.e., buying a car or a house); and collaborative negotiations, which involve ongoing relationships and business interactions. Within these types, there are three possible outcomes to the negotiation: win-win, lose-lose, or win-lose.

Either you arrive at a mutually satisfactory agreement, or someone loses—and sometimes that's both sides. Win-lose is the least desirable, for it may possibly foster a get-even attitude, wherein the loser might seek to gain something back, which can have the undesirable effect of damaging the business relationship. Win-lose negotiating can therefore deteriorate into a lose-lose game in which nobody gains anything.

The most essential goal of any negotiation is that both parties must leave it feeling satisfied that they have gotten a good deal. As we have already seen, it will involve making some concessions, but what is important is that by the end of the negotiation, both parties should emerge feeling like winners, confident that their major needs have been met.

Win-win negotiations call for meeting both the material and psychological needs of the other side.

If either side feels cheated, embarrassed, or slighted in any way—even if his or her material needs were met—this side won't emerge feeling like a winner. And that will most certainly affect any future negotiations and may impact living out the terms of this agreement as well.

Thus, it is important to preserve the business relationship. If a mutually satisfactory agreement just isn't possible, don't resort to blaming or berating or intimidation of any sort. Simply say, "I'm very sorry we can't do business this time around. It's just not in the figures. However, I'd like to give you a call the next time I need your product/service."

As you will learn in secret #16, one of your goals in planning a negotiation is to satisfy two questions: "What's in it for me?" and "What's in it for them?" When both questions are answered satisfactorily—everybody wins!

It is better to lose today's deal and keep the relationship than to take the deal and lose the relationship. Always preserve the relationship because you will need it as you live out the terms of an agreement. As time passes, conditions sometimes change and you may need to adjust agreement terms. A comfortable relationship allows these slight adjustments to be made without hassle.

THE PSYCHOLOGY OF NEGOTIATIONS

People do business with people they like and trust.

That fact is the binding element in all negotiations. If you go into a store and the sales clerk is rude or obnoxious, what is the likelihood that you will return to that store again? Pretty slim, unless they fire the clerk you don't like. By the same token, if you've made an agreement to deliver your product to a customer by a certain date and your shipping department fails to deliver on that

"Soft on people, hard on issues"

promise, you've made yourself pretty untrustworthy in your customer's eyes, haven't you?

Trust is the cornerstone of any relationship. To ensure trust, you not only have to do what you say you're going to do, you also have to understand the other party and their situation, and respond to it accordingly. In any negotiation, there are psychological needs that must be met—not just the other side's, but also your own. The psychological needs of both parties greatly influence all negotiations. Knowing how to meet those needs helps to maintain control and trust in a negotiation, and can directly lead to a win-win situation!

Remember: No one likes to feel beaten or conquered. We all have egos at stake, reputations to protect, images to reinforce, and futures to consider. Thus, the psychological needs of both parties are at least as important as the material needs. You will, in fact, find that most of the secrets in this book have to do with the increasingly important psychology of negotiating.

#6: The most effective way to negotiate

So if you know that negotiating is at least 85% psychological, and approach your upcoming negotiation with that understanding, then you are already halfway home to success. What, then, is the most effective way to negotiate? Let's take the following example:

Painter: Hi, Mr. Jones. How is the new house coming along?

Mr. Jones: It's coming along just fine. We just installed the new floors.

Painter: You know, with your busy job and the kids, you could probably use some help with all that painting.

Mr. Jones: It would be nice. But I don't have the cash.

Painter: I know it's hard when you first buy a house. But you can't overestimate the difference a new coat of paint makes! I could paint your house in two weeks, which would free you up to spend more time with your kids.

Mr. Jones: I haven't been playing with them as much as I used to. But I really don't have the money right now.

Painter: Well, I'd be willing to let you pay in installments. In two short weeks, you can have a freshly painted house and some quality time with your kids. And you won't feel the bite as much since you can spread the payments out over six months.

Mr. Jones: That seems too good to turn down. You have a deal.

Painter: Great! I'll start tomorrow, Thanks for your time.

In this example, the painter has done a number of things well. He starts off creating a personal relationship with Mr. Jones by mentioning the new house, then points out a logical fact, that Mr. Jones could probably use some help. He makes an emotional appeal when he notes that it's not easy coming up with the cash, but then points out a benefit to Mr. Jones, that he would have more free time with his children if he hired the painter. The painter goes on to appeal to Mr. Jones' values (freshly painted house and quality time with the kids), then caps the deal by giving Mr. Jones the chance to pay in installments.

If Mr. Jones had simply been asked to hire a painter, he probably would have refused, since he didn't think he could afford it. But since the painter was flexible about the payment terms and promised sincere, tangible benefits to Mr. Jones, he was able to successfully sell his services with no pressure tactics, just good psychology.

The key to the painter's success, of course, was in his ability to combine emotional appeal with logic and facts. This is without question the most effective way to negotiate! Presenting an emotional appeal opens the mind of the other party and helps to create trust. Once the trust is established, you can convince the other side by producing logic and facts that correspond to benefits for the other party. Finally, an appeal to the personal values of the other side will seal the negotiation. It's that simple!

#7: Credibility is important

To gain the trust of the other side, you have to be credible. This means that you have to be both realistic and reasonable about what you're hoping to achieve. If you go too far and ask for something that goes beyond reasonable expectations, or make unrealistic promises, then your credibility is lost—and so is the negotiation.

Let's go back to the example of our painter for a minute. If he had approached Mr. Jones and said something like, "I can get your whole house painted in three days if you pay me 50% up front and 50% upon completion?"—what would the result have been? Mr. Jones would have had himself quite a nice laugh, and never looked at that painter twice after that.

When you are in the process of setting up a complex negotiation, you will need to set limits and ranges of satisfaction. We call these limits, "Settlement Ranges" (see Secret #21). These ranges set the standards and shape the expectations by which you will be conducting the negotiation. Set your ranges too high or too low, and you run the risk of losing more than you are gaining. Remember that the other side has to trust you and what you're saying. So it is important to be realistic in determining your Settlement Ranges, and to keep your credibility intact.

#8: You have lots of power

FIVE WAYS TO DETERMINE RELATIVE POWER

1. Try to gauge your own strength or weakness. If you're strong, be sure the other side knows it.

2. If you feel you are in a weaker position, try to keep this information from the other side.

3. Gauge the other side's actual strength or weakness by examining the four leverage factors: urgency, time, competition, and desire.

4. If you feel the other side is in a weaker position, educate him or her about the weakness.

5. If you feel the other side is in a stronger position, try not to acknowledge that.

Power is a concept revered by negotiators. It is not, as the word might imply, a means of domination. Rather, it is the ability to control the situation in order to achieve the desired result. Many people fail to get very far in their negotiations because they don't realize just how much power they have. In fact, they have more than they think—as do you!

Any time you are able to craft a successful agreement, get someone to do what you want, or adroitly handle a situation so that the result is to your liking, you have probably used power. Power is not muscle. Often it is simply a subtle use of knowledge—knowledge of what the other side wants from you. No one will ever negotiate with you if you don't have something they perceive they need or want from you.

When somebody has something we want—or you have something they want—the individual with that something is the person who holds the most power. In negotiating, this kind of power is known as *leverage*. There are four factors that can create and influence your leverage:

1) *Urgency:* The person who absolutely needs something has less leverage than the person who would only like to have it. For example, if your house is flooded, you will not negotiate the price for emergency services. Most likely

POWER SOURCES

In addition to leverage, there are several other sources of power. See how many of these you use in your daily life:

✓ Legitimate power: This is the power that comes from your position, whether personal (mother, father, brother, sister, daughter, son) or professional (boss, coach, minister, doctor, nurse, vice-president).

✓ Reward Power: This comes from your ability to bestow benefits upon others (money, recognition, interesting work, important projects, etc.).

✓ Punishment Power: Your power to inflict negative outcomes upon others (exclusion from social recognition, embarrassment, uninteresting tasks, unpleasant duties, etc.).

you will pick the first company that agrees to come to your home to vacuum your water. Or if you are in excruciating pain, you will probably go to the closest emergency room. You won't call around to determine the emergency facility with the lowest cost. Urgency removes leverage from the person in need.

2) *Time:* Time pressures or deadlines generally put you at a disadvantage in negotiating. If you have lots of time, you can make sure you understand each point and negotiate at every opportunity. If you don't have the luxury of time, you have to rush through the process and may concede more than you otherwise would.

3) *Competition:* There are times when competition is a real factor and forces you to buy at any price. In a very competitive market, where demand exceeds supply, your leverage is affected if you are competing for that supply. For example, if you go to the only 24 hour convenience store open in your area, you will have to pay the prices they ask. You have little leverage unless you're willing to drive a long distance or wait until other stores open the next morning.

4) *Desire:* If there is something about the situation that has great appeal for one side, this can influence the leverage. One party wants to make the deal more than the other. The party who has a "take it or leave it" attitude has more leverage.

The two most important things to remember about leverage are: (1) Don't misuse it when it is in your favor. If you apply too much leverage, the other side often becomes inflexible or irrational, or may even walk away. (2) When you are clearly at a disadvantage, try to appear fair and reasonable, and don't betray any agitation or sense of urgency. This only increases the leverage for the other side.

But perhaps the most important thing to know about power is this: Perception is reality (see #10). If you don't believe that you have power, then you never will have it, and that's what the other side will see and believe. But if you truly believe you have power—then you do! This is why you have a lot more power than you realize—and it's up to you to use it wisely. Remember: Power does not mean you dominate; but it does mean you are indomitable.

✓ Information Power:
Private information that you may have— that is, inside information that is not commonly known.

✓ Personal Power: Your own charisma, your reputation, your stature, demeanor, how you walk into a room, your presence, etc.

✓ Referral Power: The people you know to whom you can provide access.

✓ Expert Power: Your own expertise— that is, what you know and what you are able to do; what you are an expert in, your professional expertise, your hobbies, your knowledge, etc.

#9: Personal needs versus company needs

Notwithstanding what your boss may think, personal needs are more important than company needs.

Remember, *you're* the one who is going into that negotiation, not the whole company, and you have a lot on the line when you do—your reputation, your self-respect, and the consequences of your success or failure. Besides, people need to be liked, accepted, and treated as if they were important. This is true not only for you but also for the other side. Indeed, these fundamental personal needs will outweigh any material needs dictated by either side's company.

You can use this information to great advantage in negotiating. If you can address the psychological needs of the other side by treating them with respect and making them feel valued, then you have tackled one of the biggest negotiating obstacles: the defensive posturing that can result from personal attack or irrational defensiveness, as well as a lack of respect and trust between the two parties.

It is important to remember that you're not negotiating with a company, you're always negotiating with a *person* who has individual needs, in addition to the corporate needs he or she is representing. To foster respect and trust, it is important to identify what those needs are and what kind of contribution that person is making to the negotiating process, as well as to value that contribution. Treat the other side with respect for their personal needs and admiration of their unique abilities. That will get you further in negotiating than any other tactic.

#10: Perception is reality

How you present yourself, and how people perceive you from that presentation, creates the reality of your situation.

The truth of this can be seen in a number of ways. Say, for example, you have a customer whose order has been poorly handled by your Customer Service department. Through an unfortunate and perhaps unavoidable series of mishaps, everything that could go wrong does go wrong, with the result being one very unhappy customer! Now, suppose somebody went to that customer to ask for a reference on your company. What is the customer likely to remember? The numerous occasions when a shipment went through without a glitch? The prompt and courteous service they almost invariably receive from your agents? No, most likely they will remember the one time everything went wrong, and irrationally apply that perception to your entire operation. It doesn't matter how much good you manage to do—anything negative is what they'll remember most. Or, as Shakespeare put it, "The evil that men do lives after them. The good is oft interred in their bones."

By the same token, how you present yourself at the negotiating table is likely to have a keen effect on how the other side is going to view you, and thus on the outcome of the negotiation. If you sit down and find yourself fumbling through papers, ill-prepared, hesitant, unsure of yourself, unsure of the power you hold—all of that will come across to the other side and immediately put them in a stronger position of power. On the other hand, if you arrive fully prepared and act assertively, with confidence in yourself and your position (even if it's weak!), then the other side is going to be impressed, and much more respectful of you. Inside you may be a trembling mass of uncertainty; outside you *must* be the most confident person in that room! This can have an effect not only on the other party, but also on yourself. Believe in yourself, and believe that you have power—and you will most likely find that you really *do* have it!

GETTING STARTED

No matter which side initiates the negotiation, there is still work to be done to get it off the ground. You have to understand and to prepare yourself psychologically for what lies ahead. You also have to prepare the negotiation itself—that is, take the first steps toward making contact, establishing what the negotiation will be about, and knowing whether it is even worth negotiating in the first place. And you have to establish the trust in the relationship between the two sides that will be key to bringing the negotiation to a successful conclusion.

IMPORTANT PSYCHOLOGICAL FACTORS THAT AFFECT BUYERS

✓ *Most buyers like to buy; not too many like to be sold.*

✓ *Self-interest motivates all of us.*

✓ *Most people support the status quo, or the familiar.*

✓ *Anxiety, nervous energy, or remorse often follows commitment to a large buying decision.*

✓ *Join with people and their ideas before trying to turn them around.*

#11: Your first negotiation is with yourself

Have you ever thought you were getting the short end of the deal, and that the other side was taking away more from the agreement than you were? If so, you probably felt slighted, angry, and maybe even a bit humiliated, leaving you with the feeling that you didn't want to do business with those people again. However, if you had given yourself permission to negotiate, you could have walked away with more of your material and psychological needs being met, and thus more likely to continue the relationship with the other party.

Permitting yourself to negotiate is important. By doing so, you can get beyond the concern that negotiating is "haggling" or "nickel and diming," and that you are going to be treading on toes or running the risk of being rude. Remember, the other side is negotiating, too. Just think of it as a positive process that leads to the most mutually beneficial outcome.

Successful negotiating is an important part of daily life, and in order for you to be as successful as you want to be, you will simply have to negotiate. There's no getting around it, so just let yourself do it!

#12: Make the first contact work

Since negotiating is an exchange, it begins when you make the first contact with the other side. That is when both parties have the opportunity to "size up" the other side and begin to determine what's going to happen next. That is also when both sides begin to collect important information that can be used later in the negotiation. Don't ever forget that the first impression the other party has of you will give them a lasting impression of how much power you have.

Example: A man named Peter Reilly is going to negotiate his salary for a new job. He is very unhappy in his current position, and he explained some of the reasons to his prospective boss during his interview. Unfortunately, this now puts him at a disadvantage in his salary negotiations, because the company has perceived that his needs far outweigh their own; so they feel free to offer a salary that is below his comfort zone. They hold the power, putting him in a "take it or leave it" situation—and all because of the way he presented himself in his first meeting.

First impressions, hearsay reputation, even the image of the organization for which the person works usually affects our expectations and the way we envision the negotiation process. What you come away with after the initial contact will color the way you approach the negotiation and also the way you interact with the other party. If you "read" a person as powerful or principled, you will treat him or her that way, right from the beginning. By the same token, if you present yourself in a positive, assertive manner, you will be regarded as a person with authority and treated with the respect you deserve.

Whatever Stage of the negotiation you may be in, what you say or do, either positive or negative, will affect the outcome. But the very first Stage—the initial contact—is the most crucial, because here is where true power is determined. (See also Secret #8.) So make that first contact work for you by establishing yourself at the outset as a secure and powerful party in the negotiation.

#13: Don't use the word "negotiate"

What do you think when you hear the word "negotiate?" Does it sound intimidating? Serious? Adversarial? Do you feel like you're being put on the defensive?

More than likely, that's how the other party is feeling, too, when you ask them to "negotiate." It's almost as if you're inviting them to take part in a win-lose contest, rather than a win-win cooperative effort that will meet the needs of both sides. What you really want to do is to come up with a creative, mutually beneficial solution to whatever issues you are trying to negotiate. Since that is your true goal, it helps you and the negotiation to phrase it that way for the other side, and thus put yourself on sure footing to proceed.

So try phrasing your request in a different way:

"Let's sit down and try to work this out."

"How about meeting on this next Tuesday?"

"Let's see if we can develop a solution that works for both of us."

Sounds a lot friendlier, doesn't it? Phrasing your request in such a positive way immediately establishes the teamwork attitude you need to bring the negotiation to a successful conclusion, and eliminates any suggestion of adversity. You want to work together with the other side to reach the common goal of a mutually satisfactory and beneficial agreement. So to get off on the right foot in a negotiation—don't use the word "negotiate!"

#14: Negotiate the negotiation

Before you can begin to negotiate, you and the other side have to be in agreement about what your objectives are and how the discussion will proceed. This in itself takes a negotiation!

It is important that your objectives be very clear, and also that you clearly understand the objectives of the other side. To this end, it is helpful to repeat and paraphrase what is being expressed, so that there can be no room for misunderstanding. For example, if the other party says, "I'd like to leave the meeting with a deal on this," you might respond, "So what I hear you saying is, you'd like to have an agreement on quantity and price and a contract signed by the end of our meeting." This will clarify objectives for both parties.

It is also important to discuss the agenda for your meeting. This can be either formal or informal, depending on the tone that is being set and what is being discussed. Be sure to clarify exactly what you'd like to cover in the meeting (i.e., "I'd like to discuss our pricing arrangement in terms of recent market developments.").

Be careful, however, not to turn this preliminary discussion of agenda items and objectives into the actual negotiation. Simply state what you're going to cover, and avoid value statements (i.e., "You're not paying me enough"). The idea is to simply establish what will be discussed; but wait until the meeting to start the actual negotiation.

#15: You can choose *not* to negotiate

Negotiating is a trade off in time. You have to trade your time in exchange for what you hope to get out of the negotiation. The question then becomes: Will pursuing the negotiation further really help to meet your goals, or will it simply waste your time? Or, to put it another way: Is what you hope to get out of the negotiation worth the investment of time you have to put into getting it? If not, then you can choose not to negotiate.

Let's take an example. Say you are at the grocery store, and you see that the lettuce you have picked up is a little wilted. You could probably go to the store manager and request a discount; after all, the lettuce is clearly not meeting your expectations of quality, and they will probably have to throw it away soon, anyway. So it is well within reason for you to request a lower price, right? But if you decide to speak to the manager, you'll have to find him or her first. Then you'll have to explain the problem and wait while he or she offers the discount and explains to the checkout clerk how to ring it up. You will have to spend a lot more time in that grocery store than you otherwise would. Is it worth the time to negotiate for a head of lettuce that costs one dollar? Probably not.

Of course, in real life, the situations are not always so cut and dried. If you and your spouse had a baby two weeks early and you need a crib *right now*, chances are you aren't going to want to spend 20 minutes negotiating with the salesperson in order to save $50. You need to put that baby to bed! Sometimes the circumstances determine for you whether you are going to negotiate.

There will always be situations in which you could get more by negotiating, and other situations where you may find yourself declining to negotiate on big-ticket items because you don't want to spend the time on them. It's up to you to determine whether the potential gains are worth your time. If not—it's okay if you choose not to negotiate.

UNDERSTANDING THE STAKES

You're not going to get anywhere in the negotiation if you don't understand what's at stake, both for you and the other side. There are needs to be satisfied and issues to be resolved that will affect the outcome of whatever talks you are engaged in. To enter into a meeting without being fully cognizant of what those needs and issues are is the equivalent of shooting yourself in the foot. Doing your homework—that is, having the knowledge required to conduct yourself in a secure and logical manner—is key to achieving that desired win-win situation. So,the best way to negotiate is to: analyze your needs and the other side's needs; decide what you can offer that meets the other side's needs; ask for what you need and explore alternative ways of reaching agreement. While doing all of this, create pyschological comfort by building a relationship. This formula for successful negotiation will be most effective in all collaborative situations.

#16: WIIFM and WIIFT

What's in it for me? What's in it for them? These are the two questions that will be a major concern at all times, for both sides. Whatever issue you are discussing, whatever point you are trying to resolve, you will always want to know "what's in it for me to negotiate with them?" (the WIIFM). The other side, meanwhile, will be asking themselves the same question, so it's helpful for you to know "what's in it for them to negotiate with you?" (the WIIFT). By analyzing the other side from this perspective, you are better able to ascertain their true psychological needs.

Answering these questions involves two steps: (1) You must illustrate the **benefits** of the deal to the other side; (2) You must assuage their **fear** about the outcome. These two steps illustrate the two basic types of WIIFMs: Benefit WIIFMs, where there are perceived rewards to be gained, and Avoidance WIIFMs, which tap into fears, so that the end result will prevent the fear from be-

NOW YOU TRY IT!

Try this simple negotiating exercise:

You have a car you'd like to sell. You have a prospective buyer. The car is in good condition, and the price you're asking is $5,000. The buyer is in need of a car quickly, but only wants to spend $4,000. He has test-driven your car and finds it comfortable and easy to drive. However, it is a two-door car and he really wants a four-door.

What is in this deal for you? What do you really need and want to get out of it?

What is in this deal for the buyer? What does he really want and need to get out of it?

coming reality. Fear is the stronger motivator by far, so it is to your advantage if you can determine what the fears are for the other side.

You can't even begin to negotiate unless you know what your WIIFMs are, and unless you can figure out what the WIIFTs are for the other side. You must then prepare to address both material and psychological needs in answering these questions. By taking the time to consider the real needs and desires of both parties, you'll be much better prepared to negotiate. In other words, once you have identified the WIIFM and the WIIFT of the negotiation, you can proceed to satisfy *both* needs.

#17: Identify your needs and goals

Before you begin planning for your negotiation, it is very important to have a clearly defined goal or goals. The ultimate goal can sometimes be a settlement; or sometimes an exploration of the business relationship; or sometimes it's just a means of collecting information. Whatever the goal is, the more broadly you can define it, the more likely you are to be open to creative, alternative solutions.

Take a moment to think about past negotiations, and what specifically you were trying to achieve from them. Was it an exclusive relationship with a certain supplier? Was it a lower cost-per-unit on your raw materials? Was it a commitment to a better deal for goods and services to be provided? Rather than narrowing down your goals, try broadening them. The broader the goal, the more room you have for flexibility on issues that arise, and the more likely it is that you will come up with unique solutions for resolving those issues.

Next, what are your needs? What do you want to get out of this negotiation for your side or situation? Make a list, being sure to include material needs, situational needs, and future relationship needs. Sometimes the negotiation will take more than one session, because there are multiple needs, which is something you should take into consideration when deciding on your agenda.

The material needs are the easy part; more than likely, they are tied to your ultimate goal. Material needs answer the questions "How many?" "How much?" "By when?" and so forth.

Situational needs are requirements for personal satisfaction. What do you need from the other side in order to feel a sense of personal accomplishment? It may be that you need them to concede on one important issue for you to feel successful in the negotiation. These needs are related to the goals of a win-win negotiation, where both sides feel that they've gained something through the deal.

Future relationship needs are important if you are negotiating with a long-term customer, client, or supplier. In order to preserve and further the relationship, what needs to happen in this negotiation?

Once you have clearly established what your needs are, then you are prepared to take the next step and rationally address your issues in the negotiation.

#18: Identify and prioritize your issues

"**I**ssues" are the topics you will negotiate. They come from three sources: what you want to discuss; what the other side wants to discuss; and what the two sides want to talk about. All issues must be addressed before coming to an agreement. Before beginning a negotiation, you absolutely must have a clear idea of what issues you are planning to raise, and how to make those issues part of the agenda. You also must be certain that the other party has the capacity to resolve each of your issues. Don't discuss an alternative solution that the other side won't be able to give you.

For example, if the buyer you're negotiating with doesn't have the capability or the authority to cut prices, don't focus on that as one of the issues. Focus instead on delivery time, quantity, and other pertinent issues that can be viably resolved during the course of the negotiation.

Once your issues are identified, then prioritize them. Consider them individually, and decide: How important is this particular issue compared with the other issues you will be negotiating? (See also Secret #30) Prioritizing your top three issues will enable you to focus on the ones which matter the most when the negotiation actually takes place, rather than getting tied up in issues of lesser importance. You will be able to trade concessions on the less important issues in order to retain your position on the more important ones.

#19: Anticipate the other side's needs

N ow that you've figured out what your needs are—what about the other side's? One of the most important tools you have when entering into a negotiation is information. By having as much information as you can gather about what the other side expects to get out of the negotiation, you put yourself in a more powerful position to get what *you* really want.

Of course, the other side is going to keep information from you, just as you will be keeping information from them. Chances are, their goal will be obvious, and in fact will be laid out on the table for you. Needs are another matter; but it is possible to logically "guesstimate" what their needs are going to be, and to proceed from there with your planning.

So you start with a question: What does the other party hope to gain from the negotiation? The best way to arrive at an educated answer to that question is through thorough research. Talk to people you know who have done business with them. Review any past negotiations you've had with them. Carefully consider what they could achieve through this negotiation, as well as what they have to lose. By doing this, you can reach an understanding of what will be included in their material needs.

For example, if you are negotiating with a landscaper to provide lawn service, you might consider how busy they are; how many other landscapers are out there; how their customers perceive the quality of their service; how large your lawn is (i.e., how much business you are offering them); how long they have been in business; and how their prices compare to other landscapers'. Compiling these facts will help you understand how important your business is to them and how much their service is worth to you.

When you have guessed at the needs of the other side, you can analyze how they correspond to your own needs, and thus anticipate the important issues in the negotiation. Thus, from understanding or anticipating the other party's needs, you gain the ability to anticipate the issues and to develop a strategy.

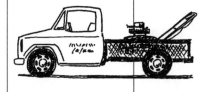

#20: Anticipate the other side's issues

Okay, so you've already guessed what their needs are. How will those needs translate into issues? The better able you are to anticipate the issues of the other side, the more smoothly the negotiation will progress. This is something many inexperienced negotiators fail to do, and they are often caught by surprise as a result.

Anticipating the issues of the other side is a crucial component of planning your negotiation. In researching the needs of the other side, you can plan your reaction to what they might bring up. For example, if you are negotiating with a small company, you know one issue that always plagues small companies is cash flow. You might anticipate that they will want to discuss payment schedules, and you can plan how you will approach that issue.

Just because you've made some reasonable guesses at what the other's issues will be, don't make the mistake of assuming that those are the only issues that will be raised. You can't enter into a negotiation thinking you know how it will turn out. That's asking to be caught off guard. Your primary concern is to anticipate issues based on what you know about the needs of the other side—and to plan your reaction accordingly.

CAUGHT UNAWARE?

If the other side brings up an issue you have not thought about, the best negotiators explore the issue (why the other side wants to discuss it; what makes it important to them; and how this issue relates to the others) and then ask for some time to consider the issue. If the other side wants to pressure you into giving an immediate response, then say, "Help me to give you a possible yes answer by allowing me the time to consider your point fully. If I have to give you an answer right now, I'm afraid I will have to say no." Most times the other side will give you the time you request. Then, be sure you consider how their request affects the remainder of the agreement.

NOW YOU TRY IT!

Return for a moment to the landscaping company described in Secret #19, with whom you are negotiating for lawn services. Can you anticipate what their issues would be? How would you approach each issue?

#21: Use a Settlement Matrix to set ranges

How far are you planning to go in your negotiation? Before you can proceed, you really need to know at what point you want to settle. This puts a sense of control into the negotiation, and enables you to know when you should stop or keep going.

Your Settlement Range can be established by means of a matrix, which allows you to sort out the issues that may have become enmeshed with each other, to clearly assess your goals on each issue separately and to remain objective and focused on these goals throughout the negotiation. The Matrix is the cornerstone of successful planning for all negotiations. It lays out, visually, all your issues, and your range of acceptance for each issue. It is important to complete the Matrix one issue at a time. The Matrix should be read vertically, not horizontally. For each issue, you need to establish four points which make up a range of acceptance. These four points are:

1) *Maximum Supportable:* This is the most (or the highest) that you can ask from the other party without leaving the realm of reason. This is your best case scenario.

2) *Really Asking:* This is what you really want to settle at for this particular issue.

3) *Least Acceptable:* This is the bottom, the lowest point you would be willing to accept and still feel you achieved a legitimate settlement on this one issue.

4) *Deal Breaker:* This is the point at which you will walk away and refuse to make any deals or come to any agreements—that is to say, the point beyond which you will not go, under any condition.

Use this Matrix to plan your next negotiation, and you will probably discover that it is a helpful tool for clarifying your objectives on each issue. Be sure to write your positions in the Matrix and remember to consider all four positions for each issue!

Here is a sample of a Settlement Matrix with four issues (in your negotiation, you may find you have more issues, so feel free to expand the Matrix):

NEGOTIATION SETTLEMENT MATRIX				
	ISSUE 1	**ISSUE 2**	**ISSUE 3**	**ISSUE 4**
MAXIMUM SUPPORTABLE				
REALLY ASKING				
LEAST ACCEPTABLE				
DEAL BREAKER				

THE DEAL BREAKER

As you get used to using a Settlement Matrix, the question may arise for you: "Why isn't the Deal Breaker just one beyond the Least Acceptable?

Answer: *The Deal Breaker is the business point at which it no longer makes any sense to do the deal.*

Example: *You may want to sell a car that you feel is worth $3,500. You know that if you donated it to a charity, the deduction would impact your taxes by reducing them $500. Thus, you advertise the car for $4,150 (Maximum Supportable); you'd love to get $3,500 (Really Asking); if you had to, you'd take $2,700 (Least Acceptable); but you'd never let it go for $500 (Deal Breaker), because you know you could donate it and at least get a "feel good" factor, knowing that it will go to some worthy cause.*

What this is actually saying is that under very special conditions, you might go below the $2,700. For instance, maybe the person buying your car will mow your lawn all summer for free, or will not pick up your convertible for another two weeks so that you can use it for a special function. Who knows what the conditions might be? But no matter what, you will never go below the Deal Breaker.

PREPARING FOR THE OTHER SIDE

How much do you know about the other side? And how well prepared are you to deal with them? *How* will you deal with them?

You simply have to be prepared. There are many variables that you are going to encounter in the course of the negotiation. You have to understand who you're going to be dealing with and what kind of conditions you are likely to encounter, as well as how to manage those conditions to achieve the goal you want. To do all that, you have to have information that will guide you and support you.

The more you know, the more power you have. It's as simple as that.

#22: It's who you know: Negotiate with the person in charge

L et's say you are negotiating with a certain company to buy one of their Super Duper Widgets. The purchase of this Widget is important to you; you absolutely have to have it by a certain date. However your budget is limited; your Maximum Supportable position is $150,000. To your great relief, the person to whom you are talking has no problems with this price, and furthermore feels certain that the delivery date you want is within reason. There's just one catch: "I have to bring this back to management for approval," he says. This is standard procedure, and to be expected—except that three days later, you hear from one of the company vice presidents: "I'm sorry, but Mr. X had no authority to make that promise to you. The terms you want are out of the question."

Back to square one. You have just wasted several hours talking to somebody who had no real power. More than likely he had been sent in to the negotiation simply to sound you out, determine what your asking price would be, and gain information on what your needs were. You have no deal and therefore no Widget, whereas the other side

EQUAL POSITIONS DON'T MEAN EQUAL AUTHORITY

You may discover that you are negotiating with someone who doesn't have the same authority that you have, even when you've tried to contact the right person with whom to negotiate. When that happens, the best thing you can do is match powerlessness. That is, discover the other person at home who has to also agree, or a boss who has to give approval on this agreement. In that way, you can both check out the agreement.

now knows about your urgency to have that Widget, which they can hold over you to boost the price up. The negotiation becomes a win-lose situation—with you in the loss column!

Similarly, sometimes the other side will claim that he or she can't make the deal without checking with a higher authority. It really limits you when the person who must give final approval is not present at the negotiation. You, on your side, have taken care of this by negotiating internally first and getting approval beforehand (#31). But the other side, being less prepared, has now stalled the negotiation, and in fact, may use this delaying tactic to get out of the deal entirely.

Whoever you negotiate with, you must make absolutely certain beforehand that he or she is the person who has the authority for that side. In a successful negotiation, both parties have to have power—that is, the authority to deliver on promises, the confidence to agree on mutual benefits, and the trust that the delivery will take place on both sides. So before you prepare for any negotiation, make sure that the person with whom you are going to deal has true power to make decisions, and can be trusted to deliver on the promises he or she makes to you—not a company lackey.

Know the identity of the person you're going to be talking to, and make sure that the person is really in charge! Only then will you have the confidence in knowing that promises made to you will not be shallow ones.

#23: Four basic social styles

Who is the person on the other side of the table? Without some basic understanding of who you're dealing with, you're like a boat without oars, forced to go where the current takes you. But if you can gain a good sense of the social style of the person(s) with whom you are dealing, you'll find yourself better able to direct that boat the way you want it to go. This is because understanding a person's social style helps you to better understand his or her needs. Social style describes a person's observable behavior only and does not attempt to uncover thoughts, motives, feelings, attitudes, and values.

What follows are four basic social styles that may help to determine the needs of those people with whom you negotiate. Most people have some of each of these elements, but we all rely on one more than the others. Once you understand the basic components of each style, you should be able to assess which type you're dealing with, and proceed accordingly:

- *Dynamic Achievers* are characterized by active, results-oriented behavior. These are the take-charge people who drive straight ahead in order to get a job accomplished. They are great change facilitators and are known to be direct and to the point.

MATCHING TO SUCCEED

Since there is only one person's behavior that you can control (and that's your own) you will want to modify your own style to match the style of the other person. Therefore, if you know a person is negotiating as a "Careful Expert," you should be prepared to discuss many details. If the person shows he or she is a "Supportive Mentor," be sure to demonstrate concern for his or her feelings and well-being. If you find you are negotiation with a "Dynamic Achiever," you may get better results if you avoid small talk, get right to the point and be direct. An "Inspirational Star" negotiator will respond best if you show enthusiasm for his or her ideas and share credit for successes with him or her.

Adding flexibility means developing situational skills and does not change the essential you; it only modifies the way you interact with a particular person or group at a particular time.

As you learn to identify people's styles and practice matching them, you will improve your rapport and communication.

- *Inspirational Stars* are the typical sales people you meet at parties. They are outgoing, gregarious, and full of energy, enthusiasm, and ideas. The Inspirational Stars love people and people challenges. They can bring people along with their personalities and they often crave social recognition.

- *Supportive Mentors* are characterized by quiet cooperation, helpfulness and support. They enjoy working with others and often coach and advise them. Supportive mentors are loyal, patient, and calm, while really caring about people's feelings. Always provide a Supportive Mentor with appreciation and with sincere interest in him or her as a person. Ask "how" questions to get their opinions and give them time to respond. Occasionally they need time to adjust to new situations and ideas.

- *Careful Experts* are calm, quiet, and detail-oriented. They live in the world of right and wrong, facts and opinions. They are critical thinkers who focus on quality, accuracy, and exactness. Always provide Careful Experts with all the details to support any ideas or suggestions you have. Don't rush them to make a decision. Let them mull over the facts. Be prepared to answer many questions in a patient, precise manner. Give them specifics.

Once you are aware of the different interaction or social styles, it will be easier for you to modify your own style to relate to the demeanor of the other person. By "speaking their language," you can—and will—create the most important element in any negotiation: trust.

#24: The solo effort and team negotiation

Are you negotiating as part of a team, or as an individual? This is an important question. After all, whom will you bring with you to the negotiating table? If you bring your boss, the negotiation will be very different than if you go alone.

Consider what you want to accomplish through this negotiation, and consider what you know about the other side. For example, it may be helpful if you bring along someone who is able to communicate with the other side more effectively than you can, or somebody who already has an established relationship with the other side. Your association with this individual will heighten your credibility and help you to create a trusting relationship with the other side more quickly than you ever could have done alone.

On the flip side, bringing somebody with you could also be viewed as "ganging up" on the other side. A one-on-one negotiation could be seen as more friendly than a team negotiation. It is definitely more personal.

Before you decide whether to negotiate alone or as a team, carefully consider the needs and circumstances of the other side, as well as the personality styles involved. Whichever strategy you think will further the relationship best is the one you should choose.

#25: Shape perceptions and expectations

Any negotiation you undertake will be fueled by perceptions and expectations—that is to say, how does each side perceive the other, and what does each side expect from the other? In order to have the most control over a negotiation, you have to know exactly what outcome is desired, and shape perceptions and expectations toward that end. Once again, preparation is key to accomplishing this.

Shaping perceptions is easy if you remember that what is perceived becomes that person's reality (see #10). Even if you are in a weaker position for the negotiation, you must take a position of strength so that the other side perceives you as really having that strength. In a way, you have to be a bit of an actor to accomplish this, but if you truly believe in yourself, you should have no problem with doing this. Additionally, what you do or do not choose to share with the other side can also shape perceptions (see #27). By creating the perception that, while you may be a nice person, you are firm on your issues, people generally will perceive you as a tough negotiator and will concede to your requests more easily - you're a force to be reckoned with.

It is also important to shape the expectations of

NOW YOU TRY IT!

Next time you're negotiating for an expensive item – an appliance, a car or some other large purchase, try making an initial offer that is significantly lower (at least 20%) than the asking price. Evaluate how the other side reacts. Do they immediately try to get something in the middle? Do they refuse to repeat your offer and counter with something just a little lower than the asking price? You might find yourself in a position to save a lot of money just by shaping the expectations of the other side.

the other side before you start negotiating. *Your initial offer will set the standard for the negotiation.* For this reason, you will experience more success if you select one issue to start the negotiation with and begin at your Maximum Supportable Level. Sometimes the other side is surprised at your offer. This only serves to create the expectation of a challenging negotiation and increases your leverage.

For example, if someone came to you and offered $50 for your $300 bike, how would you counter-offer? The likelihood is that you would probably accept much less than the bike is worth because you allowed the other person to shape your expectations—especially if you make the mistake of repeating "$50." That immediately gives validity to his or her offer, and makes it harder for you to negotiate the price to a more acceptable range. Thus, instead of repeating the figure he gave you, you should counter with, say, $300—and repeat that figure often, thereby making it the standard by which all other offers will be judged.

In negotiation, you want to be the person to shape the expectations and set the standard. Therefore you must take control: Never repeat that which you do not want to become the standard, and repeatedly emphasize that which you do.

#26: Never negotiate just one issue

I n a one-issue negotiation, there will be either a winner and a loser or two losers. It is not possible to have a win-win negotiation on one issue, because there is no room for compromise and trading.

Let's say your teenager comes to you and asks to borrow the car. At present, there is only one issue: Will you give her the car keys or won't you? You get nothing out of the deal other than a hurried "Thanks," and maybe you want a bit more than that. So you introduce other issues: "Gee, the car is really dirty. I don't know when it was washed last. And you know, every time you take the car, it always comes back with the gas tank empty. What's more, you are in the habit of changing my radio station and not putting my seat back where I like it."

Now you have multiple issues to negotiate. Your teenager will feel lucky to get out with the car if she promises to fill the gas tank and to put the seat back when she's finished. You have gotten more out of this negotiation than you would have if you had just let her take the car (in which case she would have won and you would have lost).

True, there will on occasion be situations in which you really do have only one issue to negotiate. In that case, invent some issues that you can

PLANNING THE CONTENT

When you plan the content—the substantive part of a negotiation—remember to plan the following:

✓ *Establish your goal of the entire negotiation and of this particular session*

✓ *Identify the needs (yours and theirs)*

✓ *Pinpoint all the issues (yours and theirs)*

✓ *Decide on the settlement ranges for each issue (use the Matrix)*

✓ *Set the priority of issues (your top three)*

✓ *Internally negotiate for approval before you negotiate*

give away in order to win the one you want. For example, if you really want a raise, don't just go in and ask for more money. Say: "Given my new responsibilities and the results I've delivered, I feel I deserve a promotion and a raise. Also, since I've been putting in so much overtime, I need you to grant me two weeks of compensation time. And, really, with all the traveling I'm doing, it makes sense for me to drive a company car." In this case, you can trade the promotion, comp time, and company car in order to get the raise you really want. If your boss refuses to give you a raise, you may at least walk out with a company car or some free vacation time.

The more issues you have to negotiate, the more you have to trade—and thus the more leverage you have. So cushion your "hot" issue or issues within other issues, to better your chances of winning whatever it is that matters the most to you.

#27: Information: Share and share alike—or don't share at all

A s you near the end of your content planning, you should review all the facts and pertinent data that support your side, and decide what you are going to share with the other side.

Why wouldn't you share everything? For starters, some of that evidence may be proprietary, or could possibly be used against you. For example, if we are negotiating an exclusive contract and I know there is another party interested in your services who has yet to approach you, I won't mention it. By mentioning it to you, I risk losing your interest in doing business with me. By keeping it to myself, I use that information to position my offer in such a way that having a contract with me seems to be the smartest business decision you can make. The knowledge of the other party's interest will help to shape my expectations and might cause me to make you a better first offer—but you won't know that.

However, you might just have information that is valuable to the negotiation for both sides, and the other party will appreciate your sharing it. Not only will it help both of you to make informed decisions, but your sharing of the information presents you as fair and honest.

The question might then become: When will you share this information? To answer this, you need to think ahead, anticipate how the negotiation will proceed, and consider when is the best time to bring up each big piece of supporting evidence. In this regard, it is perfectly acceptable for you to be the first to share information. After all, somebody has to go first! But it is also important that disclosures be matched, and that sharing of information is equal. If you give a little, they should give a little before you give any more.

Don't fall into the trap of giving away a lot of information about your position without getting anything in return from the other side. Information sharing should be a trade: You give a secret, and the other side gives a secret. If the other side seems unwilling to disclose, ask leading, open-ended questions. For example, if I tell the other side that I know my company needs to make this deal because we're anxious to get into a new market, I could then ask the other side, "Why they are so interested in this deal?" Force the other side to be specific by asking lots of questions.

As in other aspects of negotiation, it's perfectly okay to give something away—as long as you get something of at least equal value in return.

PUTTING TOGETHER THE PLAN

The time has come to put your plan together. A plan is your blueprint, the means by which you can piece together all the information you have been gathering and create the best, most effective means to achieving your goal. There is still a lot to do, but the more you put into the planning, the better prepared you are for the actual negotiation, which greatly maximizes your chances for success.

Probably the most crucial aspect you will have to consider in assembling your plan for the negotiation is the issues that will be discussed—yours and the other party's. Numerous decisions have to be made as to what is going to work best for you and what you are to expect from the other side, as well as how to deal with it. This involves concentration and hard work, and, as you will see, a tremendous investment of time. Time is, in fact, one of the most important factors in any phase of the negotiation process, from planning to closing the deal. How you use your time, and how you respond to the other side's use of time, will have a direct effect on the outcome.

#28: Make a business decision before the planning begins

Whether you are preparing to negotiate for your business, for your family, or for yourself, you will need to step back and assess your negotiation situation We call that, "Making a business decision."

To make a business decision, you need to know what other alternatives are available to you if you cannot achieve a settlement within your matrix. If you have many other alternatives, then you are in a strong position which is reflected in the terms of your Settlement Matrix. If this negotiation is the only alternative you have for achieving your desired result, then you need to admit this to yourself (only) and have that reality reflected in your Matrix.

For example, if you are working with a colleague on a project and you need additional time and effort from her in order to meet the project deadline, you might like to negotiate her additional effort. Now you need to make a business decision about this negotiation. Before you approach her, what other alternatives are available to you in case she refuses. If the answer is *many*, then you can reflect that strength when you set your settlement ranges. (You might be able to extend the deadline, ask a different resource, change the quality specs, or alter the scope of the project, to name a few) However, if your answer is, "None, I must meet this deadline, there is no one else who could do this work, all the work must be done at this specific quality level,"—then you are in a much weaker position and that reality should be reflected when you set your settlement range within your Matrix.

Assessing your position relative to other alternatives is what "Making a business decision" is all about.

Some people use the excuse, "I'm not a good negotiator" to avoid making a business decision. In reality, they may be fine negotiators who are unable to plan and strategize properly because they have failed to take this crucial first step. Don't be one of those people! Make your business decision before planning your negotiation, and you will find yourself much better able to handle anything that arises during the course of the talks.

SOMETIMES THERE ARE NO OTHER ALTERNATIVES!

When we bought one of our homes, the market was at its peak. After six months of culling through the newspapers (from 2,000 miles away) and calling brokers each week, one broker said that she might have a house (being exclusively listed with her) that seemed to fit our criteria. She would arrange the taking of a video so that we could see the house.

From the video, the house seemed perfect. Now we needed to establish our settlement ranges and make our Matrix. But first we needed to make an overall business decision— that is, what alternatives did we have if we could not reach agreement on this house? None, to be sure. However, instead of allowing ourselves to be in a weak position, we decided to adjust the time frame, which created other alternatives and possibilities. The result was that we negotiated as if we had several other alternatives and ended up buying the house within our Settlement Range!

NOW YOU TRY IT!

In planning for your next negotiation, consider how long the actual discussion will take. Then consciously plan for nine times that long. If the discussion will be ten minutes, plan for an hour and a half before the negotiation. If you think you are finished before the time is up, go back and review your plan. Can you bring up any more issues? Have you considered what tactics you will use? What questions you will ask? Do you know what the other side wants from you? After the negotiation, go back and review your plan. Did you cover everything you wanted to? Was there anything you should have considered in your plan that you didn't? After practicing this a few times, it will get easier for you to plan successful negotiations.

#29: Invest time in planning

By now you have probably realized how important the planning process is in achieving your desired outcomes. In fact, it is crucial to the success of your negotiation! The truth is, you should spend nine times as long in the planning phase as you do in the actual negotiation. This probably sounds like a lot of time. In the end, however, it will be time well spent.

With careful, thoughtful planning, you are ensuring that the negotiation will run smoothly. Why is this? Because you have considered and prepared for all your own issues, as well as the other side's. You have anticipated their responses and demands. You have a clear idea of exactly what you want and how you will ask for it. You will know exactly where you are willing to settle, and what you are willing to trade. You will be prepared for all the psychological ploys that will be used, and know how to counter them. In short, planning simply ensures the likelihood of a favorable outcome, so the more time you invest in your planning, the more likely you are to achieve your goals.

#30: Prioritize your top three issues from your Settlement Matrix

Once you have constructed your Settlement Matrix, decided the settlement ranges within the Matrix, and made your business decision, your next step is to prioritize your top three issues. Ask yourself, "Of all the issues I have listed, which is the most important to me?" Then ask, which is the second most important issue and the third most important issue. Using this information, you will be able to trade off other issues so that you achieve the "Really Asking" level in your three most important issues.

Thus, when you're planning for your negotiation, decide which three issues are the most critical to achieving your goal. Focus carefully on the settlement ranges for those issues, making sure they're realistic and supportable; because without the resolution of those issues, your goal cannot and will not be achieved.

It is also helpful to consider which three issues will be the most important to the other side. You have spent some time thinking about what their needs and issues might be; can you prioritize them now? If you can anticipate which three issues the other side is likely to care about most, you can plan your strategy accordingly.

Prioritizing the issues on both sides will help you to clearly see the leverage points in the negotiation. If, for example, one issue is #3 on your list, but is of little importance on the other side's list, you can be pretty sure that you will be able to trade something to achieve satisfaction on that issue.

Ideally, at least one of the other side's three most important issues won't be the same as your own. That way, you can trade and compromise so that you both reach a satisfactory agreement.

#31: Get approval beforehand

O kay, so you've identified your needs and negotiable issues. You've made a business decision by looking at other alternatives and their reality in terms of your goals. If you've done your homework, you've identified your top three issues and you've also guessed at the importance of the issues to the other side. If you haven't already done so, now is the time to put all of that into the Matrix described in Secret #21. Look your Matrix over to see if you're comfortable with it. Believe in your settlement ranges. Check again to make sure they're realistic and achievable.

When this is done, then it is time to bring your Matrix to whomever will need to approve the deal that is made through your negotiation. Pre-approval is a crucial step in the planning process; it should not wait until after the negotiation. There are several reasons for this. For one thing, you must be sure that the settlement ranges that you've established for the negotiation are acceptable within the company. Does it meet company or family needs? What effect will it have on profitability if you settle within this range, or if you concede this point to the other side? Passing it by others within the company who are directly involved ensures that you have your facts straight and have set reasonable goals for yourself in conducting the negotiation. You are shaping the

**GETTING APPROVAL
IS A NEGOTIATION**

*Gaining consensus and
getting approval on
what you are about to
negotiate and what
you will and will not
accept for each of
the issues is, in itself,
another negotiation.
Did you recognize that?
This is why some people
seek approval on only
the Really Asking, least
Acceptable, and Deal
Breaker points within
each issue. They do not
reveal their Maximum
Supportable because
they don't want to raise
the expectations of the
person who needs to
give approval. (Of
course, this always
depends on the rela-
tionship you have with
the approving person.)*

expectations of your internal people by allowing them to understand what the results will be.

Conducting internal negotiations to get approval beforehand is crucial. The ranges you have decided upon *must* be acceptable to the person giving final approval to whatever deal is made, which allows you to negotiate in good faith and with confidence in your own power. And when you have the company fully behind you, you can't help but have power!

It is also important to make absolutely certain that the people in your company who are most affected by the outcome of the negotiation are going to be able to deliver on whatever you'll be promising. You would look pretty foolish if, after you've reached the agreement, you had to go back to the other party and tell them that you can't really uphold that agreement. Such an outcome would not only disappoint and anger the other side, it would also undermine your credibility and make the entire negotiation a complete waste of time. In addition, it can permanently damage any chance of a continuing relationship with the other side.

#32: Develop your Overall Plan

THE OVERALL PLAN

When devising the overall plan for your negotiation, you should prepare for the following:

✓ *What your goals and needs are*

✓ *What your issues are, and what the other side's are likely to be*

✓ *What your settlement ranges are*

✓ *What your top three issues are*

✓ *The content of the negotiation and supporting evidence that you will present*

✓ *Any internal negotiations that must be conducted beforehand*

✓ *The tools and tactics you will use, and how you will use them*

✓ *Where the negotiations will be held*

✓ *What your questions will be*

✓ *If there is a team, what the role of each negotiator will be*

The time has come to start assembling the overall plan you will use for the negotiation. This is yet another important step in the entire process. A successful negotiation is the result of careful consideration of both content and strategy. A plan that is well thought out in advance gives you the building blocks you need to achieve your ultimate goals.

In thinking about which tactics are appropriate to use for this negotiation, consider the other party. What are their material needs? What are their psychological needs? What do they hope to achieve from the negotiation, and how does that compare to your own goals?

Now think about the issues, both yours and theirs, and determine which ones are compatible and which are likely to cause discord. You need to know how you are going to approach not just the entire negotiation but each and every issue that will be discussed. It is crucial that you make yourself thoroughly aware of what is involved, either tangibly or intangibly, in all the issues. You also need to decide upon the tone you are going to take and what your responses will be to the other side's likely objections. All of this can be determined from the information you have been so busily gathering.

Having plenty of information is key. Without it,

you run the risk of not knowing something the other side does know and can use against you. Research every aspect of the negotiation thoroughly so that you can best prepare yourself for all the possible twists and turns it might take, and have all the information and supporting evidence you need to respond intelligently to the other side's potential objections or counter-offers.

The more carefully you plan, the less likely you are to be surprised or caught off guard. The content of your plan should be as thorough and detailed as possible, to account for the goals, needs and issues of both sides, and should include all data necessary for making informed, intelligent responses to the other side. When you're done planning your content, you are then ready to plan your strategy.

#33: Plan your strategy

You have spent a considerable amount of time researching the other side and carefully considering your own needs. You have devised a strong idea of the content of your plan. Now it's time to think about the strategy you'll use. What is the best way to approach this negotiation? Will you do it by telephone, or set up a personal meeting? Will you go one-on-one, or be working in teams? Will you get right down to business, or have lunch first? Will you have a formal agenda, or merely an agreed-upon idea of what will be discussed? How many sessions will this negotiation take? Will you spend the first session developing a rapport and finding out facts, or will you bring up issues right away? In what order will issues be discussed? What sort of time frame will you use for discussing your issues? Will you be friendly and outgoing, cool and reserved or brusque and businesslike?

These questions give you some idea of all that you need to consider ahead of time in putting together a strategy for the negotiation. Your strategy is your guide for achieving the outcome you want. In devising your overall plan, it is important to consider how much leverage you have and how much the other side has, then prepare the tactics you will use to maximize your power.

The best negotiators prepare for every possible outcome so that they are not swayed by the tactics

SOME NEGOTIATION STRATEGIES

Here are just a few suggested strategies you can follow when negotiating:

✓ *Always have a rationale for any changes in your position. You need to think through your strategy so that any change in your position is supported by logic and reason.*

✓ *The smaller the incremental drop in your position, the more likely you will settle in the upper end of your settlement range.*

✓ *Save the relationship at the cost of the deal. Some deals just can't be cut. If given a choice between a very bad deal for one side or the other, or no deal at all, scrap the deal and try to save the relationship.*

✓ *Anticipate impasse; it is not necessarily a bad thing. When you hit an impasse, you can negotiate a process through it by turning it into a cooperative effort. For example, you can say, "We have reached an impasse. What can we do together to overcome it?"*

✓ *Exercise patience, patience, patience!*

✓ *Always stay aware of what Stage of the negotiation you are in and what process you're going through. Be deliberate about what you are doing, as well as how and when you do it.*

of the other side. Thus, the importance of devising a strategy that you will use for the negotiation cannot be over-emphasized! It ensures that you have covered all the bases in your planning, and will help you to focus on the best course to take for the negotiation.

One of the most important aspects of preparing your strategy is knowing in what order your issues will be discussed, and to remember that they are part of an entire package. This means that you don't necessarily want to resolve each issue immediately as it comes up. If you do that, you are left with nothing to trade when you get to the harder issues.

Secret #62 discusses the important of "cushioning" your hot potatoes alongside issues of lesser importance. Read this over and then look at the list of issues you have devised for your negotiation. Now determine what order you can put them in to give you the most effective bargaining power. You now have a strategy! (Note: The "Tools and Tactics" section of this book provides even more helpful ways to strategize your negotiation.)

PLOTTING THE COURSE

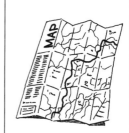

Having a plan for your negotiation is all well and good, but there are still a few strategies to consider before you can be prepared completely to enter into the negotiation. The gas is in the car; now you need to get to where you want to go, and for that there are directions to be studied...

#34: Offer to meet at their place

You may think that you would be better off if the negotiation were conducted on your own turf. But the fact is, one of the smartest things you can do is to offer to meet at the other side's place, as this gives you distinct advantages. For starters, you have saved the other person from having to travel, which emphasizes your polite consideration for others, thus putting you in a positive light. Right off the bat, they owe you for your effort. It's an easy way to get the other side to like and appreciate you.

Secondly—and perhaps more importantly—meeting at their place can give you insight into what the other side is all about, and who they really are in terms of power and authority. If you see a small, windowless cubicle piled high with paperwork and no secretary, you won't be very intimidated by the other person's projection of power. But, if the person with whom you'll be dealing leads you to the largest and most impressive office in the building—and it's his or her's—you'll be aware of how important he is in the organization.

Of course, you may go to the other side's place and be put in a conference room instead, thus denying you the opportunity to check out his office. If this happens, you still have the opportunity to check out the office building and get a sense of the size and priorities of the company itself. For example, if it's an expensive architectural masterpiece, it will be clear that you are dealing with a profitable, image-conscious company, which will help you to anticipate what their needs and issues might be.

This is not to say that you shouldn't meet at your own place. However, that option is recommended only if you're confident that it will impress the other side and you want to dominate them with a display of your power and authority.

#35: Set up time frames for discussion of issues

One of the biggest factors you have to be concerned about in conducting a negotiation is that of time—both the time spent in planning a negotiation and the time spent in the negotiation process itself. Indeed, how people use their time can play an important role in affecting its outcome, as you will see in Secret #49.

You should never give away to the other side what your time frames are for settlement; this gives them too much leverage. However, before you go into the negotiation, you should have an idea in your own mind of how much time you're going to devote to each issue. For example, if you have a two hour meeting with five agenda items to be discussed, how much time do you want to spend on each item? Of course, the most time should be devoted to the biggest issues, although these are not necessarily the first points to be discussed.

It is far too easy to spend too much time on small issues, and not reach satisfactory resolution on the larger ones. Part of your planning process should be to prevent this from happening by estimating how much time will be needed to discuss and resolve all the issues on your agenda. Then keep an eye on the clock and if the conversation gets off track, plan to put it back on course. You can say something like, "We only have a half hour left, and we haven't even discussed the pricing issue yet. Shall we move on to that?" Don't make a big deal out of it, otherwise the other side will sense an urgency that they can use against you. A gentle reminder is all that is needed to prevent the most important issues from getting lost in a bog of side issues. But remember: Negotiation is an investment in time. Don't become impatient and rush through the process.

You also have to determine what to do if you reach an impasse, and the time you have allotted to that issue has passed. How much more time you spend on it will depend on its importance to you and whether you can see a route beyond the impasse. In that case, plan for the additional time that will be needed to resolve the issue, and know what your stopping point should be before the amount of time being spent on the issue becomes disproportionate to what you would get out of the desired outcome (see #49).

#36: Know how far you will go

As we have just noted in the preceding secret, it may happen that the time you spend on resolving an issue becomes time wasted. Thus, you have to know how far you will go with a negotiation before you either concede the point or hand in the towel on the entire negotiation.

One important tool for establishing your "outer limits" is the Settlement Matrix discussed in Secret #21. If you have done your preparation, then you have arranged all your issues so that you know what your *Maximum Supportable* range is; what you are *Really Asking* to achieve; what range is *Least Acceptable* (but still legitimate); and at what point you hit your *Deal Breaker*. To put it another way, you need to have a position from where you will start the negotiation, a reasonable and realistic target for which you are shooting, a minimum you would be willing to accept for the deal, and a cut-off point, when you know for sure that no deal is possible.

Depending on the situation, there may be a temptation to take everything off the table and just go after your Maximum Supportable range. However, the danger in this is that you could damage the relationship with the other side by not giving them anything of equal value in return—and you can also end up with nothing. If you spend a lot of time working to become the "winner" of every negotiation you undertake, then you will probably find yourself to be a loser in the end, because very few people will want to do business with you. Very often the most satisfactory solutions can be found in the middle ground.

It is essential to know what your limits are. At what point do you leave the Maximum Supportable range, and move into Really Asking? How much time will you spend for discussion in the Least Acceptable range before calling it quits? How important is the issue to you? Is it worth the time you are planning to spend on it? Are the concessions you are willing to make a reasonable trade for the concessions you want from the other side? Remember: Careful consideration must be given to what you want and what you will need to give in order to know just how far you will go at any point in the negotiation.

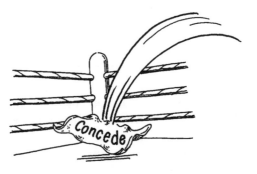

#37: Have plenty of questions ready

You have spent a lot of time preparing yourself for this negotiation. Now, as you draw up your plan and plot your strategy, you have to consider what questions you are going to ask of the other side. Then add 10 percent more questions to your list.

Why add more questions? Because they will help you clarify the position of the other side, keep you from jumping to conclusions, and give you time to prepare your response. Asking questions will force the other side to consider the logic behind their arguments and will prevent both sides from becoming defensive.

Do your best to make your questions open-ended; phrase them in such a way that asks the other side to explain, not defend. Whenever we start feeling uncomfortable, we tend to start asking yes-or-no questions that lead to defensiveness. It helps, therefore, to have plenty of open-ended questions ready in advance that will circumvent this happening.

Another powerful tactic when asking questions would be those that tap into feelings and thoughts: "How do you feel about this?" "What do you think about that?" This sort of questioning shows consideration for what the other side has to say, and that you care about their feelings.

We often fall into the trap of being so sure we're

right that we don't stop to ask what the other person thinks—and then to listen to what they have to say. In a negotiation, it is crucial that you ask questions of the other side and then listen to their answers, concerns and opinions. In this way, you demonstrate you are thinking of them and value their ideas. The fact is, the perfect solution might be only one question away!

#38: Knowing what lies ahead: The four Stages of Negotiation

Y ou have put your plan together. You have assessed the psychological and material needs of the other side. You have created a Settlement Matrix and a long list of questions. You know what issues are going to be discussed, and you're feeling pretty powerful. Are you fully prepared now? Probably. But it would be helpful for you to know just what lies ahead, especially if this is your first planned negotiation. After all, most negotiations follow a pattern, and if you're aware of that pattern, it helps you to keep track of where you are in the negotiation in terms of both the content and the relationship.

Essentially, there are four basic Stages in every negotiation, as follows:

• *Stage 1: Orientation*

Content: Introduce yourselves to each other; provide overview of why you're meeting; define the issues; mutually decide the order in which the issues will be discussed.

PRESENTING YOUR IDEAS

When conducting a negotiation, you want to present your ideas in such a way as to ensure implementation. The key to this is WIIFT— that is, what is in it for the other person to accept your idea? What makes it a good idea? Are your ideas good only to you, or do they also appeal to the person to whom you are presenting the concepts?

Whatever Stage of the negotiation you are in, you should keep in mind that an individual's response to your presentation is going to depend on his or her social style (D, I, S, or C). Thus, make sure that you gear your presentation of ideas to meet that person's needs. Otherwise, you are likely to be disappointed.

Relationship: Perform rituals and amenities (i.e., ask about family, etc.); feel one another out; set the climate for the meeting.

• *Stage 2: Resistance*

Content: Each side resists the other. This Stage is characterized by redefining issues, wrestling with personal and job needs, organizational constraints, and values and traditions.

Relationship: Both sides might exhibit fight, flight, or freeze behavior. This is the Stage of argument and debate. This is also the most tenuous Stage, as the whole deal could fall apart if you don't handle this Stage with grace and consideration.

• *Stage 3: Commitment*

Content: Both sides have pushed through the Resistance Stage and are now committed to making the deal work. This Stage is characterized by reasoning and asking questions.

Relationship: Both sides are showing creativity and flexibility, now that they have triumphed over their feelings of resistance. There is a unified commitment to a win-win settlement.

• *Stage 4: Agreement*

Content: Settlement of issues in a way that is satisfactory to both sides and results in a mutual, formal understanding.

Relationship: Both sides affirm that they are happy with the deal and enjoy working with each other. In other words: Win-win!

Of these Four Stages, Resistance is the most critical, for that is when each side will be forced to make a decision about whether they want to make this deal. If you are well prepared for objections and counter-offers (as you will be if you have correctly assessed their needs and issues), and handle yourself with a calm, reassuring attitude, you should be able to navigate through this Stage, and thus help the other side commit to the deal.

Here's a diagram of the Four Stages for your future reference:

STAGES OF NEGOTIATION		
	CONTENT/TASK	**PROCESS/RELATIONSHIP**
ORIENTATION	Introductions, Meeting Overview, Definition of Issues	Rituals, Sets Climate, Develop Rapport
RESISTANCE	Redefining Issues, Hard Bargaining	Fight, Flight, Freeze Argue and Debate
COMMITMENT	Probing and Reasoning	Flexibility and Creativity
AGREEMENT	Summary of Settlement	"It's been good working with you!"

PERSONAL PREPARATION

The day has arrived, and you're about to get in your car and head to the other side's office. You have invested a lot of time in planning for this meeting, and you feel confident that all your homework and preparation will bear the fruit you want. There are just a few more things you need to do, however...

#39: Dress for success

Sure, it's an old cliché, but never is it more true than it is in negotiations. Think for a minute about the image you want to project. Do you want to appear businesslike and powerful? Casual and confident? Humble and helpless? How you want to seem to the other side will help to determine what you choose to wear.

The other factor in your decision is what the other person is wearing. If you want to convey a feeling of alliance with the other side, dress according to what they are most likely to have on themselves. For example, if you are visiting a fishing shop to sell your bait, you will want to dress comfortably and casually—like a fisherman, not a high-powered salesman. If you are going to somebody's corporate offices, find out beforehand what the dress code is there, then dress accordingly.

Finally, remember that people will admire you if your clothing is similar to but of a *slightly* better quality than theirs. For example, when negotiating your salary for a new job, a high-quality suit subtly implies that you are worth more money. But don't shoot yourself in the foot by over-dressing in obviously expensive clothes that may imply a sense of superiority. Match your wardrobe to the environment and to circumstances, and you are one step ahead of the game in establishing your power in the negotiation.

A FEW WAYS TO DRESS FOR SUCCESS

Try this "dress code" as a guide whenever you are preparing for an important negotiation:

✓ If you want to appear powerful in order to dominate the other side (i.e., making a major purchase), wear deep, bright colors such as red or purple.

✓ If your goal is to form an alliance, wear casual business clothes. Such apparel creates trust and a feeling that you're just a "regular guy," yet still allows the other side to take you seriously.

✓ Do some homework about what the other side is likely to be wearing, and then match him or her in wardrobe. For example, if you're dealing with somebody who is very conservative, wear a dark suit; if you're dealing with an artist, wear something unique and original; etc.

#40: What you need before you walk through that door

You have now spent a great deal of time preparing for this negotiation, and you have assembled a lot of data and supporting evidence. You have organized it all and put it all together into a nice, large bundle. So far, so good.

Now, before you head out that door, review everything that you have and put to one side *only what is most essential to this meeting.* Showing up with a great pile of papers through which you have to leaf to find a pertinent document doesn't present you in the best light, does it? You should bring along only that which you *know* you are going to refer to in the course of the negotiation. Materials that will be distributed to the other side should be in a clearly marked folder (a distinctive color for the folder helps you find it easily), separate from other materials that you are planning to use for reference purposes (if needed).

Next, make sure that you have prepared the four most crucial ingredients to your negotiating plan:

1. *Agenda.* Be sure the issues are listed in the order you want them to be covered.

2. *Question areas.* What questions do you have

for the other side? Are there any details you're not clear on?

3. *Settlement Matrix.* You don't want to lose sight of the settlement ranges you established for each issue. Having your Matrix handy to refer to will ensure that you get what you really need.

4. *Support for your Matrix.* Any data or other evidence that will support your position should be organized into marked file folders that make it easy to locate the information you need *if* you have to produce it. However, keep these folders in your briefcase, and pull out only what you need when you need it. Don't clutter up the table with your files; doing so will simply clutter up the negotiation.

Finally, take a piece of paper and, with a pen, divide it into four sections. In the first box, write out your agenda. In the second box, summarize your questions. In the third box, put your Settlement Matrix. In the fourth box, list any details regarding supporting evidence—i.e., where you found the figures you're quoting, how you arrived at your offer, etc. It will help you to have this information if the other side questions your judgment at any point during the negotiation, and enable you to know just what to reach for if you have to go into your briefcase.

This piece of paper is, in essence, your entire plan, and it will be crucial to your success. Try not to let the other side see it, since it has your Matrix, and you certainly don't want them to know what your Maximum Supportable range is, versus that which is Least Acceptable. Keep this paper in front of you, but in a folder, so that you can refer to it when you need to, without allowing prying eyes to see it, as well. Guard that paper well, for it is your guide to a successful negotiation!

YOUR NEGOTIATION NOTES:

NEGOTIATION NOTES	
AGENDA	**QUESTION AREAS**
MATRIX	**SUPPORT**

#41: Prepare for the best and the worst outcomes

N o matter how the negotiation turns out, you have to be prepared for what will follow. Assume you've been amazingly successful. You've conceded very little, and the results, on every issue of importance to you, fell into either your Maximum Supportable or your Really Asking ranges. What do you do next? Well, you have probably made a number of promises to the other side on which you have to deliver. As you will see in Secret #96, your work does not end when the negotiation is ended. You have established a relationship that must be preserved, and that means making good on whatever promises you have made and following through on the agreed terms of the deal.

Thus, prepare yourself for the possibility that things are going to go well by planning ahead for the steps you will need to take post-negotiation. The faster you are able to deliver on your promises, the more you strengthen and preserve your relationship with the other side.

By the same token, you have to be prepared for what you will do if the worst happens—you cannot achieve agreement. If that should be the case, you have two choices: Forget it entirely or resort to your other alternatives (see #42).

Plan ahead for whatever the outcome might be, both best and worst possibilities, and you will be better prepared for whatever steps are necessary when the outcome becomes clear.

#42: Have a back-up plan ready

I t is entirely possible that, despite all your planning and your best efforts to reach an agreement, you still may not come to a satisfactory conclusion from this negotiation. Therefore, part of your planning should include some idea of how you will proceed should this prove to be the case. You should think about how you will implement some of the alternatives you considered while making your business decision (#28).

There is little to be gained by creating an unrealistic agreement that doesn't make business sense to both sides. Sometimes you simply reach an unresolvable impasse. Other times you realize, after a few calls or meetings, that the relationship doesn't work and you'd prefer to end the negotiation. In this case, your best course of action is to end it on a friendly note. Call the other side and tell him or her that you'll need to suspend the negotiation process because your ranges are so far apart (or whatever the reason may be). Thank the other side for his or her time.

It could be, of course, that the impasse *is* resolvable, but it may (for example) involve concessions that you had not prepared for or have no authority to make. You have to decide whether it is worth pursuing any further by going back to that person who pre-approved the desired deal and re-evaluate it internally. It all depends on whether the extra time and trouble is worth the desired result, or whether you simply have a Deal Breaker on your hands and it makes no sense to pursue it further.

Your best option is to have a back-up plan ready, in the event the negotiation fails. For instance, if you were negotiating to purchase a certain automobile and you reached an impasse on what you wanted, go to another dealer and start over. If you were looking to make a big sale to Company X, be prepared to approach Company Y, instead. By planning for a backup position, you will be able to move to that immediately instead of spending time figuring out what to do next when you can proceed no further with the current negotiation.

#43: Remember what's really important

The last thing you need to do, before you begin your negotiation, is to remind yourself of what is the most important guiding principle for you:

*Above all else, it is better to
lose this deal and keep the relationship,
than to lose the relationship and make the deal.*

Deals come and go. Needs change. Issues change. But a strong relationship will support you and your business for a long time. You never want to risk ruining a relationship for the sake of one deal.

If the other side feels hurt, angry, or manipulated at the end of the negotiation, then you have neglected your relationship in favor of the deal. Remember: a good negotiation should leave both sides feeling as if they won. Each side should get what he or she needs out of the deal. Negotiating is about creating solutions that work for both sides and arriving at mutually satisfactory compromises. It is not about domination.

Many business people sacrifice relationships in order to win a negotiation. Sure they win the battle, but they lose the war. Don't be as shortsighted as they are. If your negotiation has the potential to damage your relationship, reconsider your needs.

BEFORE NEGOTIATING CHECKLIST

Are you truly ready for that negotiation? Use this simple checklist to make sure you've covered all your bases.

CONTENT:

✓ Identified Goals

✓ Identified Needs (both sides)

✓ Identified Issues (both sides)

✓ Established Settlement Ranges

✓ Established Priorities on Issues

✓ Internal Negotiations

✓ Identified Goals

STRATEGY:

✓ Devised Overall Plan

✓ Content and Support

✓ Order of Issues

✓ Who's Negotiating

✓ Role of Negotiators

✓ Tactics to be Used

✓ Questioning Strategy

✓ Time Frames for Discussion

✓ Control of Environment

✓ Orchestration and Practice

✓ Devised Back-up Plan

You never know when you may need something from that person in the future, and if you destroy your relationship, you may be shooting yourself in the foot.

So always protect your relationship—for it is much more important than winning!

PART II

WHILE YOU ARE NEGOTIATING

AND YOU'RE OFF!

You've made it to the starting line; now you're ready to take off on your journey to the finish line. Believe it or not, the hardest part is behind you. You may still have a difficult negotiation ahead of you, but you have done your homework well, and are fully prepared to face those challenges—right?

So now that you're face to face with the other side, it is important to remember just how crucial the opening moments are in this negotiation. Everything you brought with you is neatly organized in your briefcase. On the table in front of you, you should have only a pad of paper and a pen, plus that all-important piece of paper containing your plan written on your paper pad. The crisper the environment, the more organized and confident you look, so don't clutter it up with a lot of papers.

Remember, you're in Stage 1 now (#38). You're about to size up the other side, and he or she is about to size you up, too. There will be ameni-ties to observe, and a conversation concerning what you are about to discuss—in other words, the appetizer before you get into the substance of the negotiation. A lot is riding on these first few moments. You must immediately establish yourself as a person with authority and set the tone for what is about to come. Let's take a look at how you can do that.

#44: It's all in the first five minutes

The first five minutes of a negotiation usually sets the tone for the whole meeting. All your planning and preparation for this negotiation should have already established a sense of trust and respect between the two sides; but all that will come to nothing if you don't reinforce it with your behavior during those initial minutes.

You want to be positioned to make a deal, and you won't achieve that if you go into this meeting like one gladiator facing another in an arena. Nor, for that matter, will you be successful if your attitude in that arena is that of a weak-kneed slave about to be thrown to the lions. Your best bet is to be calm, relaxed and confident. After all, you've prepared well for this meeting and are sure of yourself and your position, right? So project that attitude to the other side, and you can't go wrong.

You have done your homework ahead of time, so you should be pretty aware of who you're dealing with and what he or she cares about. In Secret #45, you will learn about matching the other person's behavior; that matching begins here, in these first five minutes. If he or she approaches you with lots of energy and enthusiasm, be sure to mirror that same energy and enthusiasm. If he or she seems serious and "all business," then you should reflect that same tone.

Now start the discussion with at least one question that shows you care about the other side as a person, even if it's just something like, "How was your drive in with all that snow?" Don't spend too much time on personal questions, however. You shouldn't do anything that will delay your getting down to business, especially if you don't know the other person. Establish the relationship by matching his or her behavior, then move on.

During the first five minutes of the negotiation you will determine the order of the issues. It is crucial for you to remain calm and cooperative, and to ensure that the other side reacts to you in a positive way. This can be done simply by showing interest in them, and doing a little probing to find out what their needs and concerns are. This sets the right tone for the entire negotiation, right at the start.

You will find that all your preparation, from determining the issues to deciding what to wear, will serve you well in these initial moments of the negotiation. A person who projects confidence and authority will be viewed with respect. And that is what you want: to create the atmosphere of trust and respect between the two sides that will establish a personal relationship between you and get you through any obstacles that may arise. By doing this, you are practically guaranteeing yourself a win-win negotiation!

#45: Match the other person's behavior

Even the most pragmatic business person makes decisions based on how much he trusts and likes the other side. Much of this is unconscious, and the reasons why we trust some people and not others might seem somewhat irrational. But the fact is, we are really reacting to the way that person behaves in relation to our own behavior.

A good way to get the other side to like and trust you is to match their behavior as much as possible. If they talk slowly, you should talk slowly. If their demeanor is direct and highly energized, then yours should be too. If they like to laugh, have some jokes ready. If their language is formal and correct, yours should be, too. If they want to get right down to business, don't waste time on pleasantries.

Personal style should also be mirrored, when possible. If the person you're dealing with is a Dynamic Achiever, then sell your position like a Dynamic Achiever. If he or she is a Supportive Mentor, then allow them time to consider the ideas and don't push for agreement immediately.

If you can mirror the other person's behavior, energy and style, he or she will see in you qualities they like in themselves. If they think you're like them, then they are more likely to relate to you and respect you. Furthermore, if each of you can anticipate and react to the other's behavior in kind, you can achieve a more balanced negotiation. To really establish a rapport with the other side, you should match them, as much as possible, in behavior, language, and style.

NOW YOU TRY IT!

In your next negotiation, or even your next conversation, pay attention to the behavior of the other person. Modify your own style to match his or hers. You might find it difficult to talk softly if your normal voice is booming, but make the effort. Evaluate the result. Do you find that the other person immediately responded to you in a more favorable way? This simple exercise can have a great effect in your everyday life. Try to mirror other people's way of speaking when you encounter them, and see the difference it makes in your relationships. Being a little bit of a chameleon can go a long way!

#46: Take notes

Yes, we all hate to take notes. It's a real drag. But the importance of taking notes during the negotiation cannot be over-emphasized, for it can mean the difference between having a definite reference and having to rely on both people's memories.

Taking notes serves two purposes. First and foremost, it is important for you to remember what was resolved and how each issue was approached by the other side. You can't rely on your giant memory to recall every aspect of your discussion, can you? Nobody's memory is that perfect, and if the negotiation goes on for several sessions, you put yourself at great risk if you don't take notes. You may remember the most important points later, but there could be crucial details that you might overlook if you hadn't written them down. Having notes also helps you later, when it comes time to summarize the agreement (see #93).

Taking detailed notes also gives you a subtle psychological edge, especially if the other side is not being as thorough as you are. Your notes give you additional leverage that you can use later when dealing with objections or formalizing the agreement. If, for example, the other side makes an important concession during the first day of negotiations, you have proof positive right on paper. Two meetings later, the person across from you makes an offer that contradicts the original concession. You remind him or her that she can't do this, because she had already agreed to, say, waive the normal 30-day waiting period before an agreement could take effect. "I never said that," she protests. "You may be right, but I think I recollect your saying that. Why don't I see if I can find it in my notes so that we can clarify this point." Then you find it and say, "I have it right here. In our meeting on April 30, right before we started discussing delivery dates, you stated that you would be able to waive that condition. Are my notes wrong, or are you unable to do that now? I'm confused." She will probably agree and you will have gotten the results you need.

However, don't lose the war while winning the battle! You might be willing to allow the other side to change terms, if it is not an important issue, in exchange for good will or a more important concession. Note that keeping your written record chronological enables you to put points in context when you have to recap something for the other side, which helps to jog their memories. It should not be used as a weapon to antagonize, as this would only threaten the relationship.

When writing down notes, try to be as thorough as possible. Note the date, and even the time when a particular issue was resolved, if that's helpful. Indicate who said what, and note what issues seemed to be important to the other side. Cover all concessions and promises made, and who made them. When it comes time to write up the agreement, you will be thankful you were so thorough, as the other side cannot possibly argue with you. After all, you have the evidence in the form of your notes!

#47: Don't confuse understanding words with understanding meaning

CUES

During the course of a negotiation, you will often find yourself dealing with "cues"—those signals, verbal or nonverbal, that may or may not be telling you something about the other side or the direction the negotiation is taking. Cues can often be ambiguous, and it is important to be careful about how you interpret them.

A Freudian slip is one kind of a cue. The other person may say or do something that sends an unintentional message about subconscious motives or feelings. Cues may also be derived from our tone of voice or the body language we use. For example, I may say, "You're absolutely right about that. I couldn't agree more." Sounds innocent enough, right? Yet if I say this in a voice dripping with obvious sarcasm, that is your cue to interpret my meaning as being the exact opposite of what I'm saying. By the same token, a certain facial expression, a shrug of the shoulders, a look exchanged with somebody else—all these can be cues that are open to interpretation.

Continued ➡

While you're negotiating, practice listening beyond the words. This is especially important when the other side is disagreeing with something you've said; it could be that he or she is really disagreeing with the way you said it, or that your words were simply misconstrued. When this happens, it is helpful to paraphrase the other person's argument, and then counter by rephrasing and clarifying your position.

As an example, let's say that you ask your assistant to photocopy 30 documents by noon. She says, "That's not possible. There is no way I can get all that done by noon!" This gives the impression that she is being argumentative, or is unwilling to help out; however, it may simply be that she has a lot of other work to do and finds it difficult to take on another task. Considering that possibility, you reply, "So you feel you can't do it? I realize you are very busy, of course. But this is an important assignment, and I understand that you will have to put your other duties aside in order to complete it. If you don't worry about the phone and your other work, do you think you could get it done?" Chances are she will see the logic and

It is important to note that nonverbal cues are common only within certain cultures or sub-cultures. With so much cultural diversity in negotiating, caution must be taken not to attach too much meaning to a particular cue or nonverbal action. You may be perfectly right in your interpretation of certain cues—but you may also be wrong, and that can lead to misunderstandings and possible damage of the relationship. So take care how you react to cues in a negotiation. If you're not sure what a particular nonverbal cue means, describe it to the other person and ask for a meaning or what the person was thinking. If you cannot develop an understanding through discussion, you will have to resort to observation and assumption.

importance behind your request, and will accept the assignment.

What was important in this situation was that you did not interpret her words to mean one thing rather than another. What you might view as a lack of cooperation could be a simple matter of somebody feeling overwhelmed by work and being understandably unwilling to take on another assignment in addition to everything else she has to do. By listening beyond the words, and clarifying the meaning that she could put everything else aside, you paid attention to her needs and found a quick resolution to the problem.

Differing points of view are a normal part of any negotiation process. But you can deal with them more effectively if you focus your attention on meaning, rather than just words. It helps to remember that the true meaning is not in the words—it's in the relationship.

#48: Don't play games

There are many common negotiating tactics with which you will become familiar, like little ritualistic dances that will leave you out in the cold if you don't know the steps. You may perceive these tactics and strategies as forms of game playing. The truth is, they are simply a means of making you aware of what is going on.

Tools, techniques and tactics—shaping perceptions and expectations—matching the other person's behavior—using certain words and phrases—all of this may be construed as a form of game-playing. In fact, each day, we all behave in certain ways to elicit particular responses for others. These actions are, in fact, beneficial to a relationship.

The types of games I'm talking about are those that set out to deceive the other side, and abuse the trust that you have worked so hard to establish. If your goal is to create a win-win situation, then such games will only damage the relationship, as well as reduce the likelihood that you will ever negotiate with that person again.

Nobody likes to feel tricked. If somebody makes a promise to you, then reneges on that promise by making a better deal with somebody else and forcing you to renegotiate, how would you react to that? More than likely, you would never want to do business with that person again.

Lies, deception and trickery have no place in honest negotiations. Integrity, morals, and a positive reputation are still highly valued commodities, and should be pursued at all costs if you want to be respected as a negotiator. So avoid any games that might jeopardize the relationship—and your reputation!

———

HELPFUL HINTS

#49: Time should be on your side

We have already talked about the importance of time in planning your negotiation. Now let's turn our attention to how you can make best use of time *during* the negotiation.

Time can be a powerful ally. If you have lots of time, and can stay engaged in working through all the issues and ideas, you greatly increase your chances of coming away with the deal you want. If you don't have the luxury of time, you generally have to rush through the process, which puts the other side in the driver's seat. If they're aware that you are under time constraints, they can hold that over you to force concessions from you that you might not ordinarily make.

As discussed in Secret #35, it is helpful to set up time frames for discussing your issues. You can only go so far before the need to achieve resolution on a certain issue becomes no longer worth the time and effort you have been pouring into it. However, you should not reveal to the other side any deadlines or time pressures that you may be under, as this will put you in a less favorable position. Exercise patience at all times, and never display any urgency to resolve an issue. Always remember: The person who has the least amount of time generally loses.

But what if you do have a deadline that you have to meet? Then it is important to keep in mind that the other side probably has deadlines, too. You can use time as a negotiating tactic to force resolution on certain issues. For example, you could say: "We agreed to resolve this issue today, but we are running out of time. Can we agree to X?"— then state your position. The time pressure may force the other side to agree to your terms. However, this tactic is best used on smaller issues. You don't want to force agreement on really crucial issues. At best, the deal will fall apart, and at worst, the relationship will suffer because the other side feels he or she has been manipulated. Use time to your advantage, not to your disadvantage.

#50: Negotiate the whole package

On the surface this may seem to be obvious advice. After all, you're aiming to achieve a particular goal, and that encompasses your entire package, does it not? Yet it is surprising how many people create problems for themselves by focusing too much on individual issues. Yes, we've placed a lot of importance on issues in this book, and yes, you need to treat each issue separately most of the time. But the point is this: *Negotiate all the issues first, before settling any one of them.*

If you settle each issue independently, then you will find yourself with nothing left to trade at the end. By putting all the issues on the table first, you are better able to trade those that are less important to you for the ones that are important to you. Remember, the goal is to settle the entire package, and you can only do that if all your issues are out there.

Let's say you're buying a house, and the issues of negotiation are the price, the settlement date, the furniture in the house, and who will pay for the new roof the house needs. If you bring these up individually and first decide on the roof issue, then decide on who gets the furniture, by the time you have to settle the price, there is nothing left to trade! But if you start off by saying up front: "We have four issues to resolve here: The roof, the furniture, the settlement date, and the price," you set yourself up for a much more agreeable package deal. You might offer to pay for the new roof if they throw in the furniture in the house, and you'll agree to settle a month earlier than you'd like if they knock the price down $3,000.

Putting all the issues on the table at the beginning of the negotiation makes for more creative solutions and happier negotiators. Each party is more likely to walk away with what he or she needs if the issues are discussed as a package and used for trading, rather than settling them independently.

#51: Share information at the right level

Information—having it and using it—is an important tool in your negotiating arsenal. You will collect information about the other side, and you will also assemble data that will support your position. Sometimes you may even gather crucial details that will affect the outcome of the negotiation—details that you may or may not choose to share with the other side. (See Secret #27.)

You will need to understand how the development of a trusting relationship brings with it various levels of information sharing. On what level of information sharing are you operating? There are three basic levels:

- *Public:* This is the sort of information that is common knowledge, or at least easy to obtain. You would have no problem with sharing this sort of information with anybody. For example: "Sales were down 25% last quarter."

- *Private:* This is what you *really* think. You could share this with your boss, but it would take a while (and a whole lot of trust) before you would share it with the other side. For example: "Sales were down 25% last quarter, and I think it's because our new brochure missed the market."

- *Intimate:* This is "grapevine" information that results from speculation or gossip. The likelihood of your sharing this sort of information with the other side is slim, unless you have managed to build a close and trusting relationship. For example: "Sales were down 25% last quarter, and I heard that it's because the new marketing manager screwed up the brochure."

It is very important to know on which level of information sharing you're operating in a negotiation. Trust and a rapport with the other side will move you from public to private to intimate information—but move slowly. The critical thing is to match the level of the other side. If you go too far into the private realm before they do, you could wind up saying more than you wished to.

Remember: You can't take it back once you've said it. So if you say what you really think, don't say any more until the other side tells you what *they* really think.

#52: Don't be afraid to ask for what you want

This is a fundamental secret in negotiating! It is amazing how many people stop themselves from asking for what they really want because they figure the other side would never agree to it, or would be unable to provide it. Well, you never know unless you try—so don't be afraid of trying.

Sure, the other side might say no to your request. So what? That is the risk you take in negotiating. One of the goals in any negotiating process is to address the needs of both sides. This can never happen if the necessary information isn't shared. Therefore, it is your responsibility to make the other side aware of your needs so they can be addressed in the negotiation.

Remember, negotiating is a give-and-take process. In order for the other side to give you what you want, you have to tell them what that is. You'll never get something if you don't ask for it!

NOW YOU TRY IT!

Think about your last negotiation. Was there something you wanted that you didn't ask for? Try to determine how important it was to you and why you didn't ask for it. How do you feel about it now? In retrospect, do you think the other side would have conceded on that issue? In your next negotiation, prepare a list of everything you want. Bring up each item regardless of whether you think the other side will agree to it. You may be surprised at what you'll end up getting!

#53: Make sure the other person wants what you're offering

In any negotiation, each side will have issues that they are willing to give away. You have, in fact, already learned the importance of having extra issues to discuss that aren't very important to you, so that you can trade them for something of real value. Of course, it's important to know whether the issues you want to concede are all that important to the other side in the first place!

Thus, before you make a concession in a negotiation, make sure that the other side values that concession. Let's say you just bought a house and you need a lawn tractor for your new lawn. You see one at the hardware store with a price tag that says $2,999. That's a lot for you to pay, since you just spent your life's savings on a house. Your lawn is only half an acre, so you don't need a big mower. The salesman offers to throw in a free trailer, but you still don't budge on the price. You don't need a trailer, you need a lawn mower. Since he offered the trailer, you'll take it, but you still want the price to come down.

The salesman made the mistake of offering you something you didn't value. He loses a trailer and still has to come down on the price to sell you the tractor. Before offering you the free trailer, he should have asked whether you were interested in any accessories. He might have discovered that you really needed a leaf blower attachment, which he could have offered you at a much lower cost instead of the trailer. This would have pleased both sides, and may have satisfactorily concluded the negotiation.

Before offering any concession, determine if the other side would value that concession. (see #'s 55 - 59 for more on Concessions)

So whatever you are willing to concede—make sure the other side will really want it!

#54: Friendly persuasion: Selling is asking, not telling

A s you have gathered by now, the process of negotiating is very much a process of selling. In effect, you are selling your position to the other side, which in turn means you must persuade them to buy what you're offering. The key word is "persuade," which does not mean telling—it means asking.

Successful persuasion depends on your ability to convey the benefits of what you're selling, logically relating those benefits to facts and features that will appeal to the other side. Then the other side must draw his or her own conclusions. For example, if you have a product you'd like the other person to buy, he or she will want to know how he or she could benefit from this product. You state the features of your product, relate them to the benefits they can provide to the individual, then ask the other person if he or she agrees that these benefits are important and worth the purchase of your product. In this way you are asking the person to come to his or her own conclusions; you are not telling them or forcing them.

The same holds true for any type of negotiation. In selling the other side your position on each issue, state the benefits to them and to their company and ask for agreement. Be sure the other side desires these benefits both for themselves and their organizations. You always need to provide a rationale and some facts so that it seems logical, but facts and logic, by themselves, don't usually persuade.

In this way the other side is forming its own conclusion rather than feeling pressured. Asking questions that lead them to a logical decision is what successful persuasion is all about.

It is helpful to know that persuasion is accomplished when three factors intersect:

1. When, on the emotional level, the individual understands that it is in his or her best interest (and in the best interest of the organization) to behave in a certain way.

2. When the action or idea can be supported with reasons, facts, or logic which "makes sense" to the individual.

3. When the action or the idea can be reconciled with the person's value system.

Thus,

Emotion + Logic + Appeal to Values =

Persuasion!

THREE STEPS TO PERSUASION

Successful persuasion involves three basic steps, all designed to guide the other side to a logical decision:

1. The claim: *This step appeals to the other side's emotions. You make a claim (i.e., "This is the best paint you can buy") which will create interest or an emotional response in the other person ("Oh, really? Why is that?").*

2. The fact: *This step appeals to logic. You back up your claim with a substantiated fact or information ("Because it covers even the darkest colors in one coat and cleans up easily with water").*

3. The benefit: *This step appeals to values. You link your claim and your fact together to create a benefit for the other person ("So you can paint your living room in just one day, instead of spending your entire weekend painting").*

By clearly stating and linking a claim, a fact, and a benefit, you will find that you are much more successful at persuasion than you have ever been before.

THE ART OF MAKING CONCESSIONS

As you have already learned from Secret #3, every negotiation involves concessions. A person who insists on sticking to his or her Maximum Supportable range at all costs is somebody who is going to be disappointed in the end. If the goal is a win-win situation, then you have to accept the fact that give and take will be the means to achieving that goal.

Don't assume your needs and those of the other side are in conflict. (If the needs were to be in direct conflict, success in the negotiation would be very slim indeed.) In most cases, the needs are not conflicting and a win-win solution can be achieved through discussion, understanding, and developing alternatives. If you understand the negotiation process, take my word for it, both parties can get what they want. Both win!

#55: You scratch my back, I'll scratch yours

Making concessions in the process of "give and take" is an inevitable part of negotiations. However, your goal is to get what you need out of the negotiation. This means that you should never give up anything without getting something in return.

Because the relationship is important, care must be taken in how you do this. After all, the other side is after the same thing you are: a fair and reasonable trade on issues so that you both come away winners. Thus, pay attention to the language you use and the way in which you present your concessions to the other side. Phrase your concessions like this: *"If I were to* pay what you're asking, *would you be willing* to sign a five-year contract?" In other words, *ask* the other side to give something of value to you in return—don't *tell* them.

If each concession is communicated as a trade, you will reach agreement faster and both sides will feel that the negotiation was a fair one. Never give a concession without linking it to something you want in return. If you make all the concessions first, and then have to go back and ask the other side to make some concessions, the equality of the trades becomes ambiguous. You won't be sure that

---

DO NOT MAKE OFFERS OR CONCESSIONS WHICH DO NOT MEET NEEDS

One of the most common mistakes in negotiating is making offers and concessions that do not meet the needs of the other side. There are three reasons why this happens so frequently:

1. The needs of the other side are not obvious and those involved in the negotiation process don't take the time or make the effort to uncover the true needs.

2. The obvious needs are not necessarily the real needs. Sometimes requests for certain concessions are only symptoms of the real needs. When this happens, it is the responsibility of the requesting party to be sure he or she is asking for what is really needed. In the absence of precision, the other party needs to check to be sure the concession does meet a real need.

Continued ➡

3. Sometimes we're just not listening well enough, and make unwarranted assumptions. Many times one side will make an offer or concession that he or she thinks the other side should want; or they make a concession which they would want if the sides were reversed. The problem here is that the offer or concession is aimed more at the needs of the maker than at the needs of the receiver.

To rectify any of the above situations, the two parties would be better served by spending more time in the probing and listening process, rather than in working to formulate offers and concessions.

the trading was fair. For example, if you agree to allowing your teenager to borrow the car, and then ask her the next day to wash it, don't count on a definite yes. She may or may not wash it, depending on what her busy schedule allows. After all, she already got what she wanted yesterday. Trade at the time the favor is requested. In that way, you can be more sure of the results.

Remember: Concessions must appear to be fair and equitable trades, so that both sides have gained something.

#56: It's okay to make the first concession

S ometimes negotiations can reach a stalemate simply because neither side wants to be the first one to "give in" on an issue. They are afraid that doing so will make them seem weak or over-eager, and that their power in the negotiation will be negatively affected and give the appearance of defeat. As a result, both sides dance around each other, unwilling to make the first concession. This wastes a lot of time and energy and results in no issues being resolved and a complete lack of productivity.

But concessions aren't about victory or defeat; they are about moving the negotiation forward so that both sides can win what they want in the end. Thus, don't be afraid to make the first concession if it will help to get the ball rolling in the right direction. Just take care that you don't offer a number too far from your opening position.

When it comes to the first concession, what's really important is *how far you drop from your first offer*. Remember that when you start out, you are working in your Maximum Supportable range. Whatever you concede, it should only be a small, incremental drop from that range. For example, if your Maximum Supportable is $100, and what you're Really Asking is $75, you shouldn't drop to

$75 in your first concession. In order to get as much as you can from the negotiation, try dropping to $99. That shows that you're willing to negotiate—but you're going to be tough!

Making the first concession is okay as long as you don't give up too much in that first round. It's better to make the first move and keep the negotiation going than to waste time waiting for the other side to concede first.

#57: Never concede during the Resistance Stage

The Resistance Stage of the negotiation is the time when there will be a lot of discussion and debate about the issues. It is most definitely *not* the time to make concessions!

This will be difficult, because this is the point in the proceedings when you will feel the most pressure to make a concession. You can expect there to be disagreements; the other side may, for example, claim that you're unreasonable, and that your demands are outrageous. The deal may be put at stake, and they may be threatening to walk out if you don't back down. Nevertheless, hold your ground, and do not concede anything.

Resistance is to be expected, not feared. Your goal will be to get the other side through the Resistance Stage and toward a commitment to an agreement. What you want is a win-win settlement, with both sides committed to making the deal work. If you make a concession while the other side is still resisting you, you'll only be giving in to appease an emotion, not to trade something for something else. Additionally, if people recognize they can use emotion to pressure you, they will have found a strong tactic which may leave you in a position of weakness, and perhaps feeling resentful by the end of the negotiation.

Remember, you get through resistance by asking questions, remaining calm, and trying to find mutual interests.

Commitment to working things out and formulating an agreement, *follows* passage of the Resistance Stage. To ease the way from Resistance to Commitment you will need to explain your position, make an effort towards understanding the other person's feelings, and ask questions to explore the other side's concerns. Do not appear judgmental, and do not feel obliged to rationalize your position. Simply continue to ask the other person to explain his or her feelings and objections, listen attentively, paraphrase what they are saying, and above all, remain calm. If you demonstrate concern and probe for interest from the other side, the chances are good that they will move beyond the Resistance Stage and into the Commitment Stage. And once both parties are committed to making the deal, the reasoning and trading begin. The important point to remember here is: Never give a concession during the Resistance Stage!!!

#58: Never concede under pressure

We have already seen the importance of time and how it can be used in affecting the outcome of a negotiation (Secret #49). Bear this in mind as you go along, because you must be prepared for the possibility that the other side will use a deadline as a tactic to pressure you into making concessions you are possibly not yet prepared to make.

Deadlines force action and pressure people into an "either/or" choice. Many people use deadlines, either real or imaginary, to force the other side to concede. This is the sort of pressure that you must resist. If the other side tells you that you have to reach an agreement by a certain time, probe to determine whether that deadline is real. Ask questions—for instance, "What happens if we miss that deadline?" This can help you to determine whether it is an actual deadline or just one fabricated to pressure you.

If you can't figure out whether the deadline is real, you'll have to work within its constraints. The best way to handle the pressure placed on you is to make the other side share that pressure. For example: "Well, if we have to reach agreement by 4:00, we'd better resolve these issues. Are you willing to give up the exclusivity clause in exchange for me reducing my price?" Make the other side a party to the importance of the deadline. If you have to reach agreement quickly, both sides should have to concede.

It's okay to make concessions to meet a deadline, but the other side should match your concessions. If they won't, then you're better off walking away from the deal.

#59: The best concessions to make

There are two concessions you can make which will cost you nothing. They are *patience* and *listening*.

Think about how much you appreciate it when someone really listens to what you're saying or when they take the time to explain what they mean. It makes you feel respected and cared for, doesn't it? Patience and listening are powerful tools in a negotiation, and what's best is that they are concessions which cost you nothing.

It doesn't cost you anything to hear the other side out. Listen to what they're saying and take the time to ask questions and communicate your own ideas. This may be difficult if you're naturally impatient. If that should be the case, you must learn to discipline yourself and to recognize the importance of paying attention to the other side.

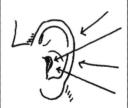

Patience and listening are the two concessions that will always be valued by the other side. These two tools will help to create trust and respect, and will ultimately allow you to reach an agreement faster. If you're not willing to take the time to listen to what the other side is saying, then you can very well end up at an impasse that will slow down the whole negotiation process.

Therefore, try not to be in a hurry to reach an

agreement. The time you spend listening and asking questions will be time well spent!

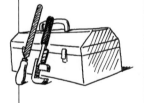

TOOLS AND TACTICS

It should be clear by now that conducting negotiations involves forethought and planning. You and the other side will be sparring partners as you hammer out an agreement. There will be discussions, there will be concessions, and there will be trade-offs. But none of this simply "happens"; often a little bit of help needs to be applied in the way of a tactical strategy.

To achieve the goal you want, you have to use certain tools to get there. You have already applied some of those tools in the sidebar work you have done, and chiefly by your study of the other side's material and psychological needs. You can use the information you have gained to choose the tools and tactics you will actually use to conduct the negotiation, specifically as you discuss and decide the issues.

It is important to remember why you are using these tools and tactics, which is to move the negotiation along to achieve a mutually satisfactory settlement—*not* to play tricks on the other side or to gain the upper hand over the other side. Never forget that the relationship is paramount, even at the expense of the negotiation!

#60: Write it down

Secret #46 demonstrated the importance of taking notes during the negotiation. But there is another use for that pen and pad of paper in front of you; it can be employed to reinforce your position and make your Really Asking goal a reality.

It's simple, really. Just put a blank piece of paper between yourself and the other person. Then, as you negotiate, write down the things that come up which are favorable to your position.

For example, say that you are negotiating the purchase of ten computers and you want a certain price. You say: "I propose to buy ten computers at $1,000 each." Then write those figures down on the paper. If the person objects, simply respond, "Let's just write things down as they come up so we don't forget." Chances are, that person won't write anything down—you're the one with the paper, after all, and you've already noted the figure—so that by the end of the negotiation, you have a list of points that are favorable to your position. Because these points now exist in writing, they become the standard by which you are operating, which in turn forces the other side to give credence to them.

Everything becomes more real when it's in writing. Most likely the other person had a figure of $3,000 in mind, but that seems ridiculous next to the $1,000 on the paper. Thus, he or she will most likely counter with something much lower than his or her original figure, putting you in the driver's seat to achieve your Really Asking price.

Make sense? Try this in your next negotiation and see what happens. Did the other person write anything down, or were you the only one with that piece of paper, listing the points that you would like to use as the standard for negotiation. Now look at the agreement that resulted from the negotiation. How close did you come to your Maximum Supportable range?

Writing things down can be a powerful tool. Don't be afraid to use it!

#61: Repeat only what is to your advantage

Perception is reality; and that which is repeated, either aloud or in writing, also takes on a reality which can make it the standard for the negotiation. Therefore, it is important to avoid repeating any figure or position taken by the other side, especially if it is not advantageous to your own position.

Let's explain this. Let's say you're trying to arrange delivery of a purchase for Friday of this week. However, the store's policy is that they need ten days. If you continue to repeat, "this Friday," chances are that the store's counter-offer will be formed using that day as a guide. But, if you start working from their ten-day point and begin to repeat that number (thereby reinforcing it as the standard), you probably won't receive your delivery on Friday. If you don't repeat the other person's unfavorable number or term, you stand a better chance of getting what you really want.

This secret is especially helpful if your Maximum Supportable Range and the other side's Maximum Supportable Range are very far apart. By not allowing the other side's figure to become the standard, you better your chances of settling the negotiation closer to your own standard.

So if somebody throws out a number you don't

NOW YOU TRY IT!

Try this the next time you're negotiating. Offer something that you know is far from what the other side really wants, and repeat your offer several times. Don't repeat the other side's offer. After you reach agreement, determine how close you came to your Maximum Supportable range. See how easy and powerful this little technique can be?

want, never repeat it and never write it down. In short, don't accept any figure or position that could become the standard against which you might have to negotiate.

#62: Cushion your hot potatoes

Throughout this book, we have discussed the advantage of having multiple issues to discuss. Arming yourself with numerous issues gives you more you can use for trading purposes, and greatly increases your chances of winning on those points that matter the most to you.

Let's examine how this works. Say you have identified the three issues that are the most important to your position. These are your "hot potato" issues, one or two of which may prove to be especially difficult. In addition to these, you have two or three more issues that have some value to you, but are not critical, and another three or four that don't matter to you in the least—in fact, you created those issues as give-away items. In determining the order in which you are going to discuss your issues, cushion your hot potatoes within the other issues so that they can absorb the impact that your hot issues are going to make.

It is helpful to bring up the most difficult issue early, but not too early. Start out with something easy, then put something difficult on the table, then go back to something easy, and so on. In this way you work in your hot potatoes among the other issues; in essence, you are concealing that which is most important to you.

Now, as the negotiation progresses, the smaller, less important issues can be used for your gain. If you concede to the other side on those issues, then they feel like they're winning overall, which will make them feel magnanimous when it comes to settling the hot potato issues you want to be resolved in your favor.

Thus, in your next negotiation, don't identify your larger issues. Simply cushion them with the less important issues, and see what results!

GOOD COP/BAD COP

A tactic you are likely to face during a team negotiation is the "Good Cop/Bad Cop" routine. This is where one person plays the bad cop, always taking a tough stand, while the other person will be reasonable and friendly. The idea behind it is that, after hearing the unreasonable or un-suitable demands of the bad cop and getting no place with him/her, any demands that are put in a nice tone and seem reasonable are likely to be accepted. This is a common way of nego-tiating when two or more people are in-volved on a side. When used on you, this ploy can have the undesired effect of your making more concessions than you planned, just to reach a "comfortable" agreement. Here, there-fore, is how to counter-act this tactic:

Continued ➡

#63: "The Krunch"

"T he Krunch" is a simple but powerful tactic. One party simply says, "You have got to do better than that." When most people hear this, they tend to eliminate some of the extra they had added to their offer. They are happy to get a second opportunity to make another offer after the other side has, in effect, threatened to walk away.

You can use this tactic to great advantage, especially early in a negotiation. It signals the other side that you really mean business. It subtly implies that their offer is unreasonable, without putting them on the defensive. It really is a great tool!

If you're on the receiving end of this tactic, acknowledge the request and reply by asking them to clarify what exactly they mean and where they need you to do better. For instance, if you offer me $200 for my refrigerator and I counter by saying, "You've got to do better than that," you can try offering $210—a very small concession. Another alternative is that you can link your concession with something you want from me—i.e., "If I can do better on the price, can you pick up the refrigerator so I won't have to deliver it?" Just don't allow me to intimidate you into giving away more than you should. If I really want you to buy my refrigerator—which you assume that I do—then I'm really more flexible than I'm letting on!

1. First, be prepared for this tactic to come up whenever you're involved in a team negotiation. It's especially likely to happen if the team members are a boss (who plays the bad cop) and his/her subordinate (who becomes the angelic and accommodating good cop). This way, the subordinate can preserve the relationship by being the nice guy, and blaming his/her boss for any and all uncomfortable decisions that are made.

2. Next, try to separate them. Set up the negotiation with just one player and make it clear that the other person is not welcome at the table. This is effective, but not always possible if they absolutely insist on negotiating as a team.

3. Finally, and most effectively, force them to agree before you continue the negotiation. As soon as they pull out the good cop/bad cop routine, don't play along; just step back and say, "You two need to agree on your position before we can continue," and then refuse to negotiate further until they're in agreement. This takes the wind right out of their sails!

#64: "The Straw Man"

O ne way of ensuring that you get what you need on the important issues is to include additional issues that you really don't care about with the ones you feel are important to you. These issues are "straw men" that distract the other side. You argue strongly for one of the less important issues, and then finally give in on it. The other side feels that they have won a point, and are more likely to give in on one of the issues that are more important to you.

The key to success with this tactic is credibility. The other side must believe that your straw man is really an important point. If they suspect that you are using this tactic, the game is over.

If you plan to use this tactic, it would be helpful if the other side has an issue that is less important to you, but very important to them. Since the other side cares a lot about that issue, it will be easy for you to convince them that you do, too. You can pretend that the point is of critical importance; then, when you concede on it, the other side will be grateful. Of course, this tactic does not work as well if your straw man is of little importance to the other side.

What if this tactic is being used on you? If you suspect that one of the issues being hotly debated by the other side is really a straw man, you should probe for its importance. Ask questions, such as:

"What would the consequences be if you don't get what you need on this issue?" and "How does this rank in importance with all your other issues?" Let the other side know that you are concerned about their priorities in the interest of arriving at an agreement that is best for both parties. This is the easiest way to keep a straw man at bay.

#65: "The Bogey Tactic"

An often effective negotiation tactic is the bogey, so named because it involves making an offer that is just under par. For example, if I'm selling a car priced at $20,000, you might say: "I love this car, but I have only $18,000." You are stating a fact (or at least what I have to assume is a fact), which encourages joint problem solving. If I really want to sell you that car, I'll have to work with what you can afford to pay.

This is one of the best tactics you can use, because it doesn't result in defensive justification or competition. You present your offer in terms of your limitations, not in terms of how much you think the product is worth. In fact, you may think the car is worth only $18,000, and that's why you're offering me that much—but I don't know that. If you had told me right out that you would pay only $18K because that's what you think the car is worth, I would most likely have gotten defensive and prove to you why it's really worth $20K.

Starting a negotiation this way leads to creative trading. I might, for example, sell you the car for $18,000, but you'll forego the CD player and leather trim options. We can make trades this way until we're both happy with the deal.

Unlike some of the other negotiating tactics, this one is not likely to arouse suspicion in the other side. By praising their product, you are endearing yourself to them, and they will probably want to work with you. It is even more effective if you can compare their product to someone else's. For instance, you could say, "I like this car much better than the Toyota down the street. But I only have $18,000." This lets the other side know that you are aware of your options and are willing to walk away if they can't figure out how to work within your limitations. Chances are, they'll make the deal you want.

#66: Sweeten the pot

When you're nearing agreement, one way to get closer to your Really Asking figure is to use the "Sweetener for the Pot" (also called "One More for the Road") tactic. This allows you to extract one more small concession before closing the deal by saying, "Just throw in X and you've got yourself a deal."

Let's say you're buying a man's suit. You've gone back and forth on the price with the alternations and the discount. You are close to an agreement. You're happy with the deal, and you'd be satisfied with it. However, by using this tactic, you could get a little more. When you accept their final offer, you could say, "Just throw in the tie and you've got yourself a deal." Chances are the seller will be happy to include it in order to close the sale.

Using this tactic also communicates to the other side that accepting their price is a concession on your part. By asking them to throw in something else, you're telling them that their offer is just shy of meeting your needs. It's likely that they'll want to make the deal, and by asking them to throw in something small, you make it easy for them.

Try using this tactic in some of your negotiations. Don't always walk away when you have what you want; just ask for one more small concession each time. The worst they can do is say no—in which case, you graciously accept the offer, again communicating to them that it's a concession on your part, which makes the other side feel like a winner. This is a classic win-win situation.

OTHER PLOYS AND TACTICS

Here are some other tactics you may encounter:

*1. **Deadlines:** Deadlines force action. They pressure people into making an either/or choice. You can never be sure the time limit is real, yet you can also never predict the cost of not meeting that deadline.*

*2. **Deadlock:** Similarly, declaring an impasse or deadlock when the negotiation isn't going your way is a threatening technique. When declared in earnest, it either indicates that Settlement Ranges don't overlap and there is no deal to be made, or it demonstrates a lack of interpersonal skill to handle disagreements.*

*3. **Springing a Leak:** Leaked information can be very valuable for your negotiations. Arrange for the information to get to the other side indirectly. In this way, you can increase the credibility of your stand. When you stumble upon a leak from the other party, be sure to test out the source before believing it.*

*4. **Ignorance:** This is a tactic that offers many benefits to the person courageous enough to use it. In his essay "Of Negotiating," Francis Bacon tells us how hard it is to negotiate with a man who is indecisive, disorganized, foolish, or fanatical about his viewpoint. Sometimes it's okay to be confused and unaware.*

Continued ➡

#67: Play humble, play helpless

Sometimes there is an unequal distribution of power in a negotiation, and you might find yourself negotiating with somebody who has a lot more leverage than you do. This can happen for a variety of reasons—for example, the other side might have something you need very badly; or you might be new to the business and at a disadvantage because of your lack of experience; or your position in the market is smaller and weaker than the other side's.

If the other side has all the power and you have almost none, one very effective tactic you can use is the humble-and-helpless technique. Bare your soul and be humble. Tell the other side that you have to make this deal or you will be fired, broke, or whatever dire consequences await you. Ask for the other side to help you out, to give you a chance to redeem yourself. Give them the opportunity to do you a favor. They will usually show surprising magnanimity.

This works in part because you are flattering the other side by admitting that they have all the power and that you need them. People like to feel needed, and they like to be in control. The humble-and-helpless approach also gives the other side a chance to show their spirit of generosity. In most cases, they will welcome the opportunity to appear powerful and generous and will give you a break.

WORDS, WORDS, WORDS

Words comprise one of the most powerful tools in your entire negotiating arsenal. In fact, words can make or break the negotiation. A deal can fall apart completely when the wrong word or phrase is used. Conversely, the right words can clinch the agreement and ensure a happy ending to the negotiation.

In Secret #47, you learned the importance of not confusing the words that are used with the actual meaning of what the other person is saying. Words can be deceptive. They can cut to the bone, and they can soothe and calm ruffled emotions. They can tear apart relationships, and they can bring people together. In short, words are power.

In this section, you will learn a few key words and one phrase that can have an important effect on the outcome of your negotiation. Weaving these words into your discussion will often dictate the course of the relationship. Try them out, and see for yourself!

5. Red Herring or Decoy: These are two diversionary tactics designed to turn the attention of the other side to an issue or action that is less detrimental than the one they may consider. Brer Rabbit, caught by the fox who most probably would eat him, proclaimed, "Please don't throw me into the briar patch." As a result, thinking this was the worst thing he could do to the rabbit, the fox threw him into the briars, where he was, in fact, perfectly at home—and the fox couldn't follow because he was afraid to enter that patch himself. This is a decoy. The red herring plays the same game, except that you agree to give in for a price. Using the same example, if the rabbit agreed to enter the briars by himself for a price, that would be a red herring.

6. Walk Away: This tactic has a legitimate place at the negotiation table. You need to know your "Deal Breaker," and when it is reached, you should walk away. This tactic is sometimes used as an empty threat to raise anxiety in order to pressure the other side into giving in. Such a "take it or leave it" attitude is risky, and can adversely affect the nature of the relationship.

7. Withdraw an Offer: This tactic is especially risky, but it can be used successfully at the ending of a negotiation. You are generally close to settling an agreement and then you change a term and feign necessity to withdraw an offer. It forces the other side's hand and will either make or break the deal.

#68: Magic word number 1: "Unfortunately"

- "I really wish I could join you today. Unfortunately, I can't be there until tomorrow."

- "I appreciate the offer you made. Unfortunately, this car is worth a lot more than that."

- "I'd like to be able to oblige you. Unfortunately, I can only give you a discount if you buy six pairs of shoes."

The word "unfortunately" is one of the most powerful words you can use in negotiating. You should use this word when disagreeing with the other party, or refusing to make a concession in a negotiation. "Unfortunately" allows you to disagree with the other person while at the same time showing empathy for his or her needs. By using this word, you remove any hint of contention from the relationship and, instead, put yourself on the other person's side.

Say, for instance, you are negotiating a new employee's salary. Rather than just saying, "There's no way we can pay you that much," say instead, "I really wish we were in the position to pay that much, unfortunately, we aren't." Now, instead of putting the employee on the defensive about his or her abilities and value, you are implicitly agreeing that he or she is worth the figure, and that you wish you could pay him or her more, but that you're limited by your company. This eases the pain of disappointment for him or her, and makes it less likely that he or she will respond angrily.

By using this one little word, you show that you are working as a partner with the other side to arrive at an agreement, not as an adversary. Take a look at the three sentences with which this secret began. Compare them with the following:

- "I can't be there tomorrow."

- "This car is worth a lot more than that."

- "I can't give you a discount unless you buy six pairs of shoes."

See the difference the word "unfortunately" makes? It magically adds empathy to the relationship, and certainly makes life easier for you by a long shot. So keep this word in mind and use it when disagreeing. By doing so, you'll find that the other side will be much more receptive to you.

#69: Magic word number 2: "Need"

"**N**eed" is another powerful word to know and use. It conveys the importance of your request or demand without being either too officious or too timid. "Need" is a potent tool to use when phrasing your desires. Even if the something you want from the other person doesn't fill an obvious physical or material need, employing this word will make what you're asking for seem critical in nature.

Here are some examples. Notice the difference between the impact of the first and second statements:

- "I have to have more money."
  "I need more money."

- "I would like to have this by Friday."
  "I need this by Friday."

- "I want to have an exclusive agreement."
  "I need an exclusive agreement."

The differences may seem to be subtle, but they are important. In the first examples, the reaction to your statements might be, "Yeah? So what?" But when you use the word "need," it implies that you won't make the deal if you can't get that concession. Even if that's not true, when you concede on that issue, it will be much more powerful than if you act as if it's not really important to you, or if you couch your request in more timid terms.

Everything you ask for should seem of critical importance, and should convey the impression that it's absolutely necessary to you. That way, the other side will think they can't force you to give in as easily. Using the word "need" fits the bill nicely!

#70: Magic word number 3: "Uncomfortable"

When you need to disagree with the other side in a negotiation, try to phrase it using the word "uncomfortable." People have a universal understanding of how important it is to be comfortable, and most will go out of their way to avoid making others feel uneasy or uncomfortable. By phrasing your disagreement in terms of your own discomfort, the likelihood is that the other side will rush to make you comfortable again.

Thus, rephrase your disagreement or objection:

Instead of: "I can't agree to that," say "I'm uncomfortable with that offer."

Instead of: "I don't like that solution," say "I'm uncomfortable with that solution."

Instead of: "I don't care for the design," say "I'm uncomfortable with the design."

Phrasing your objection this way lets the other side know that they have the power to make you comfortable again—which they will probably do by making some kind of a concession. The use of this word also brings the negotiation to a more human level. Comfort is universal and understandable, and by saying you're uncomfortable you will elicit sympathy rather than defensiveness from the other side.

#71: The magic phrase: "Help me understand"

These three little words probably have the most power of all when it comes to breaking an impasse. Using these words will make the other side feel that you need their knowledge and expertise to understand the issue. Additionally, the information they provide will help you to clarify the meaning and to respond to it appropriately.

One of your jobs in a negotiation is to make the other side feel important, right? By saying "help me understand," you are telling them that they know something you don't, and that makes them feel that you respect and value them. They might then be more open to persuasion for your point of view.

Therefore, when you disagree with something the other person has just said, start your objection by saying: "Help me understand how you reached that conclusion" or "Help me understand why you feel that way." This ensures that you truly understand where they're coming from, and also gives them a chance to rationalize their position. They may even realize an error in their thinking as they explain it to you.

Most important, "help me understand" tells the other side that you need their help, which makes them feel smart and powerful—and more likely to

FINDING MORE NOTEWORTHY WORDS

As you observe people in meetings, on television, or in negotiations, listen to not only what they say, but also how they say it. Begin a word list of your own. Capture phrases you like or particular words that seem to be effective. Be on a "word alert" as you go through your day. Begin to expand your style by adding words and phrases that you think make you more effective.

be magnanimous when it comes to making concessions!

#72: The taboo word: "But"

All the words we've discussed in this section are quite powerful, and have a positive connotation for your negotiation. However, there is one small, three-letter word that is equally powerful, but in a negative way. That word is "but." Amazingly, using this word can defeat all your efforts to build a strong relationship with the other side. Let me show you why.

If I say to you, "I understand what you're saying, *but* I just can't make it work," how does that make you feel? Like I don't really understand what you're saying, after all? That's because the word "but" completely negates anything that went before it. It is construed as argumentative, not cooperative.

Here's another example. Let's say we are working together on a project and you have what you think is a great idea for presenting it to our boss. You say, "I have a great idea. How about we write everything in pink marker so that it stands out?" I reply, "That's a good idea, *but* pink won't show up as well as red."

So what did I just say? It seems like I didn't really think it was a good idea, and I was just pandering to you. That probably makes you feel that I'm insincere and might make you resent me. At the very least, it will make you think twice before you tell me another one of your ideas.

When you have a difference of opinion with somebody, what you want to do is demonstrate a cooperative attitude rather than an argumentative attitude. Suppose I had said: "I like your idea of using a color that stands out. What do you think about using red, since it's a bit darker and stands out even more than pink?" Phrasing it this way gives you credit for your idea and makes a suggestion in a positive way.

Being cooperative and respectful rather than argumentative is what you want to strive for in a successful negotiation. You will find it difficult to remove the word "but" from your vocabulary, since you've probably been using it all your life to disagree. It might be helpful to write yourself a little reminder on your notepad—i.e., "NO BUT"—before you start negotiating. Then, when it comes time for you to voice a disagreement, you'll be more conscious of your word choice.

#73: Rephrase, to offer your suggestion

There are times when you need to disagree with a particular point that the other side is making. You might want to do that by offering a different suggestion. You could say, "No, I don't think it should happen that way," and then go on and give your own point of view. However, you could also just rephrase what the other person said in a way that includes your point. Here's how that would sound:

The other person says, "I think you should prepare the order and send it out while I work on getting the purchase order through."

This is definitely not okay with you since you will be incurring costs to prepare the order, ship it out for delivery (more costs) and you don't even have a purchase order, much less a deposit.

You could say, "Let me see if I understand your suggestion. You're saying that I should get everything ready back in my company so that it's ready to be built and shipped immediately upon receipt of the purchase order. Is that right?"

You will find the other person usually responding with, "Yes, that's that I meant."

This is a nice way to avoid a long discussion about the sequence of events.

THE PSYCHOLOGICAL EDGE

Using certain words in certain circumstances is just one way you can give yourself a psychological edge in a negotiation. There are many other subtle and useful techniques you can learn that do not manipulate, but rather allow you to control the negotiation, and to keep yourself from being manipulated by others.

Always keep in mind the importance of preserving the relationship. You don't want to steamroll over the other side. You want them to feel important and successful, while at the same time protecting your position and achieving your goals. This involves having some psychological tools at hand that you can draw out of your bag of tricks as they are needed. Here are just a few that will help.

#74: The effectiveness of body language

As we discussed in the Sidebar of Secret #47, it is important to remember that until you know a person, no nonverbal cue can be interpreted with one hundred percent accuracy. In fact, not even a smile means the same thing all over the world. So don't rush your judgment about a person just because she's slouching or he's grimacing. These sorts of things mean different things to different people.

That said, how can body language be effective in negotiations? For starters, you can deliberately create an impression of rapport with the other side by matching them in dress, speech, and posture. By mirroring the other person's body language, you can create the perception of harmony and mutuality.

Your own personal body language will inevitably send signals—usually unconsciously—to the other side. Because they can be misinterpreted, you sometimes have to be conscious of the signals you're sending out. Do you drum your fingers when you're impatient? Do you make a face when you hear something you don't like? Do your eyes light up when you hear something you do like? Do you scratch the tip of your nose when you're trying to conceal something? All of these nonverbal

TELEPHONE NEGOTIATIONS

Using the telephone to nego-tiate has its pros and cons. Without the visual element that exists when you're talk-ing to somebody in person, it is a lot easier to mistake or misinterpret the tone of voice or the words being used. Phone negotiations hold the advantage of speed—you won't be tied up in a meeting for two hours—but also the disadvantage of requiring more frequent calls to settle a deal, plus the possibility of distractions while you are on the phone.

When negotiating by tele-phone, you will find that it's better to make telephone appointments, just as you would if it were a regular face-to-face meeting. This practice will help eliminate that missed call or haphazard conversation which may lead to grave consequences.

It is also very important to listen. While you can't see the other person's face or see any gestures, you can still judge a lot by the tone of their voices and how they react to you. Use pauses and silences to help gauge that reaction and to gain useful information or even a concession; silence generally tends to make people nervous and they will blurt out things to fill it.

Finally, be sure to write up a memo or letter summarizing the results of your telephone negotiation. Having some-thing in writing helps to clarify what you talked about and establishes what agree-ment you came to so that both sides understand it.

cues are likely to be noted by the other side, and whether their interpretation of what your body lan-guage means is correct or incorrect, it can still have an effect on any decisions they make.

You may be trying to figure out what the other side has in his or her hand. You, too, should be monitoring body language; just be careful how you interpret what you see. After all, a scratch on the nose may be just to satisfy an itch, nothing more. What this means is that there are times when you may want to consider checking the meaning of a concerned look or a shake of the head with the other side. You might ask, "I notice you seem to be frowning. Could you help me understand if you're concerned about something?" Or: "I notice you're shaking your head. Is that in response to some-thing I'm saying, or are you thinking about some-thing else?"

Finally, what sort of impression are you mak-ing? Are you sitting up straight or are you slouched in your chair? Do you look a person straight in the eye, or do you tend to glance away when speaking to somebody? This last habit is something that is particularly important to correct. Most people find it disconcerting when the other person doesn't look straight at them. It can be in-terpreted as a sign of evasiveness, as if you have something to hide. Hold yourself erect, with con-fidence, and look directly at a person when you're talking to him or her. Your posture, your face, and even how you use your hands—all these con-tribute to the nonverbal signals you are sending out. Try not to give them anything to misinterpret!

#75: Make silence your ally

Face-to-face negotiations and telephone negotiations should be handled with the same care; and in both cases, silence can be one of the most potent tools you can use. Think about how you feel during long pauses in regular conversation. Now think about how such pauses can be used to your advantage, whether over the telephone or in person.

For example, if the other side makes an offer that you don't like, pause for a long time before responding. This puts the other person on edge; he or she might be thinking about how you're going to react, and how he or she will react to your reaction. He might even jump in with another offer before you respond to the first one, just to break the silence.

Silence can also be used to show that you're contemplating all the options. When you're silent, you appear thoughtful and careful, which makes the other side think that you are more difficult to manipulate.

In telephone negotiations, silence is even louder. Since the other side can't see your expression, silence can be that much more unsettling. Be aware of this when you're negotiating by phone, and plan your pauses accordingly.

Sometimes the other side will use silence against you. Be prepared for this possibility, and

---

TEN SUREFIRE TELEPHONE NEGOTIATION TIPS

Once you're aware of the limitations of negotiating by telephone, you can adjust your negotiation strategy accordingly...

1. Prepare for every call. Outline your strategy beforehand.

2. Schedule the telephone negotiation so that the other side can prepare for it, too.

3. Clear off your desk to make room to work. Have everything you need ready, including your Negotiation Matrix!!!

4. Take complete notes on every conversation and date them.

5. Be specific, and be sure to repeat key points.

Continued ➡

6. Don't keep people waiting on hold or hanging on during long pauses. If you have to do this, then apologize and explain the reason for the delays.

7. If you are unprepared for something the other party has thrown at you, don't try to deal with it immediately. Say you'll call back, then get all the details you need before you do so.

8. Don't negotiate an issue to its conclusion until you fully understand it and have a prepared position and are ready to settle an entire package.

9. Allow sufficient time before concluding the negotiation; don't rush it just because you're on the telephone.

10. Don't be afraid to reopen an important issue if you realize that what you agreed to doesn't make sense after you hang up the telephone.

don't let it rattle you, especially now that you know that deliberate silence is a negotiating tactic. Don't rush to break the silence. Try to show the other side that silence doesn't bother you; in fact, you relish it as an opportunity to think. If they see that it's not disturbing you, they will probably abandon the tactic.

Not only does silence give you time to collect your thoughts and plan your next move, it can also make the other side more willing to concede on an issue in order to break the silence and move on. If, however, you sense that it's affecting the comfort level of the relationship, then fill the silence by explaining what you're doing. Silence should be a tool—not a weapon.

#76: Be a good listener

L istening is more than just hearing what the other person is saying, without interrupting him or her. There is an art to listening that is very easy to learn and can have very positive consequences on the outcome of the negotiation. Good listening is *active* listening—that is, absorbing and assimilating the person's thoughts before responding to them.

The secret is this: Pay close attention to what the other person is saying, then pause to paraphrase and summarize his or her key points when he or she is finished, *before responding to what was said*. This is active listening, and you can demonstrate it by nodding, jotting down notes, and, most importantly, looking directly at the other person while he or she is talking. It is crucial that you show interest in what the other person is saying, and really think about it. Before you jump in with your own thoughts, take a few seconds to summarize what you understood the other person said. This, in itself, helps you to clarify what your response will be, and will allay any misunderstandings ahead of time.

For example, if I told you that I think we should cancel our vacation and just relax at home because there's so much to do before we leave, you could respond, "So what you're saying is that you feel stressed by the preparation which, of course, will be over when we are on the plane tomorrow morning." Paraphrasing what the other person said is a good way to check the meaning and to ensure that you understand what he or she is saying.

Active listening effectively demonstrates your respect for the other person's ideas and allows you to work creatively at an agreement. If you listen well to the other person, he or she is more likely to listen to you. So it is a good idea to hone your listening skills in an active and positive way. Good listening makes for a good relationship!

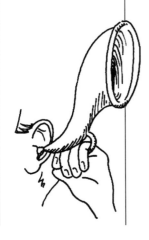

#77: Agree before you disagree

In Secret #84, you will learn the importance of preventing hostility before it creeps into a negotiation. Yet there are bound to be disagreements; nothing ever goes so smoothly that two sides won't have a single point of contention. So how do you contend with disagreements in such a way that hostility is kept at bay? Well, first of all, you have to remember that carelessly rejecting somebody else's ideas is a sure guarantee for destroying the trust and respect you have worked so hard to build.

So what you must do is adopt the habit of agreeing before you disagree. First, listen with genuine care to what the other person is saying. Acknowledge that he or she might have a point. Find the truth in what they're saying; agree with that; and then voice your disagreement.

The best method for applying agreement to your disagreement is to use questions. Here's an example:

"What I heard you say is that you think we should take Route 78 West instead of 80 North because it will be quicker. Hmm. I agree that we want to take the quickest route. But do you think that 78 will be quicker, even with all that construction?"

As you can see from this, it helps to summarize what the other person is saying, and to use a pause before you voice your disagreement. The key is in

A MODEL TO DISAGREE

1. Listen as though you care. Don't stop listening and don't interrupt the other person as soon as he or she says something with which you disagree.

2. Summarize both feelings and substance. Paraphrase what the other person said, both in content and the way he or she feels about it.

3. Pause contemplatively. This shows that you're giving the other idea some thought.

4. Agree with something the other person said. Even if it's something minor (such as the Principle behind the statement), find something in his or her argument with which you can agree.

5. Pause. Again, you're demonstrating that you're carefully considering the idea.

6. Disagree, using questions to gently point out the logic of your position.

the use of questions. This forces the other person to logically evaluate his or her position as well as yours, and will thus lead you to the right solution. It's better for the relationship if that person thinks she solved the problem herself by answering your questions, rather than being dominated by your logic. No one likes to be wrong, no matter how persuasive the arguments might be. Asking questions gives the other side the chance to be right, without trampling all over his or her point of view. So always find some piece in any statement that you can agree with before you disagree.

#78: Use the 4 F's to handle objections

MODEL TO JOIN THE 4 F'S

F eel
(So you Feel .....)

F elt
(Others have Felt .....)

F ound
(They Found...)

F ind
(You may Find ....)

There are several ways you can handle objections in a negotiation, but the most useful way I have found is a powerful tool called the, "The 4 F's: Feel, Felt, Found, and Find." This tool is used to deflate defensive posturing, avoid hostility, and persuade the other side of the strength of your position. Instead of becoming overly defensive about your offer, you join the other side in their reaction to the problem, and in so doing, work out a creative solution.

Let's say you're talking to a building contractor whom you have hired to put on a new roof. He wants to do the job for $4,999, but you think the job is worth $3,500. He is objecting to your offer, and you use the 4 Fs to manage his objections, as follows:

Roofer: "I absolutely cannot do that job for $3,500. It will take me three days and three men to do it, and I'll lose money if I do it at your price!"

You: "*So you feel* that the time required to do the job prevents you from lowering your price. *Others have felt* that way about some work they've done around here, too. *They found* that the promise of two week's work at this time of year was worth reducing their price a little. *You may find* that your business will be better off if you do my roof for

$3,500, rather than having to scout around for another job this late in the fall."

By summarizing the roofer's position and telling him that he's not alone in his concerns, you are joining him in his reaction to the problem—although you're not agreeing with him, you're simply working on his side to persuade him of the logic of your offer. In effect, you are telling him that it has worked for other people and it might work for him; but you are doing it without becoming defensive or hostile about your logic. The idea is to convince, not to browbeat. The 4 F's will help you do just that!

#79: Be soft on people—but hard on issues

Sometimes the person with whom you're negotiating will annoy you. Sometimes he or she will frustrate you, or just plain make you angry. We've all had situations where a negotiation turns into a shouting match, or, worse, a stalemate because of hard feelings on one side or another. What's important to remember when this happens is that your goal is not to *win*—your goal is to *reach an agreement.*

Too often we get caught up in the need to be right, to prove to the other side that we know better than they do and are therefore the "winners." But what happens when both sides are vying to be right? *Nothing!* And when nothing happens, that is when resistance and resentment take over, and the negotiation falls apart.

So what should you do? You can't back down on issues that are important to you. But you can keep the negotiation focused on reaching a solution by keeping your emotions in check if and when the other side starts to frustrate you. Separate your feelings about the person from the issues. So it's okay to be tough on the issues; but treat the other person with respect and consideration as you do so. For example, if you need to disagree with the

TEAMWORK

Most times you're on your own in a negotiation; but sometimes you'll be working with a team (see Secret #24). Team negotiations can be time-consuming, but sometimes more creative solutions are reached as a result of the additional people involved. Here are some tips for success when teamwork is involved:

1. Matching: As a rule of thumb, if the other side is negotiating as a team, you should negotiate as a team. Otherwise they will have the chance to "gang up" on you and put you at a disadvantage. Conversely, if the other side is sending in just one person, don't come surrounded by an army yourself. Know ahead of time whether this will be a solo effort or a team negotiation and plan accordingly.

2. Selection: Pick the best people for the job. For instance, if you're negotiating something technical, make sure a technical expert is included on the team. You can also match people's interests and styles—i.e., if the other side has somebody who likes to sail, bring along the guy who taught sailing camp in high school.

3. Planning: Team negotiations require a little more planning to ensure that everyone is working off the same page. Make sure that all team members are clear on the goal of the negotiation and the strategy you'll take.

4. Consensus: Before you go into the negotiation, it is important that all team members are in agreement about goals, strategy, tactics, and settlement ranges. You also need to reach a consensus at the conclusion of each issue and before presenting each offer. This is why team negotiations can take longer than one-on-one negotiations.

5. Strategy: One advantage to team negotiations is that you have more room to strategize. You can plan who will bring up what issues, who will disagree with the other side, whether you will play "good cop, bad cop," and whose job it is to watch the time and keep everyone on track. There should be a clearly defined role for each person at the table, and one of those people should be taking notes.

Remember that a team is very much like an orchestra. You are the conductor, and the other people on the team are the instruments that you bring in and direct. So it is important to know who is playing what and to have harmony among your players. Be clear on your planning and your strategy, and you are sure to create a Negotiation Symphony!

other side, disagree with the substance of what he or she is saying, not with the person. Instead of saying, "I think you're wrong on that," try saying instead, "That solution doesn't meet my needs." By directing your disagreement at the issue and not at the person, you can prevent hurt feelings and resentment.

When the shoe is on the other foot and the other side says something that hurts your feelings, acknowledge the comment, but steer the conversation back to the issues. For instance, you could say something like, "I'm sorry you feel that I'm not capable of making this deal work. Help me to understand why you need X..." This lets the other person know that you're paying attention to him or her, but that you're not willing to get sidetracked from important issues.

As we have stressed time and again in this book, it is most important to remember that you want to *preserve the relationship* with the other side while getting what you need from the negotiation. If you can remain respectful and considerate of the other side while being tough on the issues, you can achieve that goal!

#80: Ask the other side for help

A sking the other side for help can turn out to be a powerful tactic you may use in your negotiation. This does not mean that you want to present yourself as being helpless. Rather, you want to involve them in coming to a creative solution to a problem. By adopting a cooperative rather than a combative attitude, you are showing respect for the other side's contributions.

Think about it for a moment. Who knows better than the other side how far they will go? If you get them to work with you in looking for an agreeable settlement, the brainstorming that results may bring about a solution that will surprise and delight you. "We seem to be at an impasse. Maybe I need to understand your issues better. Please help me to do that." This is one approach you might try. Another one: "Please help me to see why giving you such a reduced price on those lots will be beneficial to me."

Asking the other side for help is most useful when you reach an impasse in the negotiation. If it just doesn't seem as if you'll ever reach agreement, invite them into joint problem solving. Suggest that you put your heads together to try to arrive at a solution to the problem. By asking for help, you are in effect joining forces with the other side, which makes the chances of a mutually satisfactory agreement that much better.

HIGH ANXIETY

No matter how well you prepare for a negotiation, no matter what tactics you use to anticipate and deal with the various psychological aspects of the meeting, no matter how diplomatic you are and how hard you work to preserve the relationship—the time will probably come when tension will get high and nerves will get on edge. Sometimes, for instance, it doesn't matter in the least what you know about the four basic social styles; you could very well come up against somebody who just plain sets your teeth on edge, or who is (you realize) a dishonest, unscrupulous individual. When that happens, you cease to be dispassionate about the other side; a personal element creeps in, like it or not. For that matter, the person on the other side may take an instant dislike to you for no obvious reason, and that dislike mars or even prevents any logical, reasonable conclusion to the negotiation.

Taking something personally, over-reacting to something that is said, tension, defensiveness, even hostility—these emotions can all be part of the negotiating process. The trick for you is in recognizing what is happening when it happens and dealing with it then and there, rather than allowing negative emotions to take over the negotiation. Here are a few secrets for maintaining your calm when everybody around you is losing their heads.

HOW TO COUNTERACT STONEWALLING

When the other side starts stonewalling you, they are relying on provoking your anxiety and forcing you into making concessions just to move the negotiation forward again. Here are some steps you might take to counteract this tactic:

1. Be aware of your own patience level. Are you really being stonewalled, or are you simply being impatient? Keep tabs on the state of your patience; it is in your own best interest to do so.

2. Recognize that this tactic may be even more difficult for the other side than it is for you. He/she must be feeling impatient by now, and stonewalling can be very tiring. You can use this to your advantage.

#81: Control your emotions

Easier said than done, you say? It's simpler than you think! Remember that the negotiation table is no place for a display of unplanned or unwarranted emotions. Even if it means sacrificing the deal, it is more important for you to save the relationship; so you should never become so defensive, hostile or frustrated that you start shouting or crying or having any sort of a temper tantrum.

But let's face it—it can take a pretty concerted effort to keep your emotions in check, especially if the other side doesn't. If he or she is combative and argumentative from the start, it will take some serious self-restraint to prevent yourself from responding in kind.

So what can you do to keep your emotions in check? For starters, it helps if you have your plan on paper, and nearby, where you can check it regularly (see #32 and 36). This serves as an effective reminder of why you're there—specifically, to work together to arrive at a mutually satisfactory agreement.

Secondly, know when to take a break. When feelings are getting pretty hot, insert a pause to help everybody cool down. Ask the other party if he or she minds if you excuse yourself. Walk around the building. Get a cup of coffee. Take a deep breath. Do anything you need to do to focus your mind on the purpose of the negotiation, and not on any perceived slights or insults.

Sometimes a break can release tension and give both sides a chance to calm down and regroup before returning to the negotiating table. So when it seems that emotions are taking charge of the negotiation, take charge of the emotions by taking a break. By doing so, you will probably find both parties more amenable to striking a deal after the cool-down period.

3. Consider setting a deadline. You could say, "If we can't reach an agreement by the end of the hour, the deal is off." This lets the other side know that you won't give in under pressure—you'll walk away, instead. If that happens, you'd both be stuck, so the chances are good that he or she will come around.

4. Openly consider the advantages of coming to a decision. Emphasize how beneficial it would be to both of you to reach an agreement. Get him or her to agree that making this deal is important.

5. Prepare your own people back home for a long negotiation. You don't want pressure from your own side, too; therefore let your office know that this might take a while.

6. Consider walking out. But assess your options first: What are the consequences of not making the deal?

#82: Patience is a virtue—but it's also a weapon

We have seen how silence can be a very effective tool in forcing one side or the other to make a move (see #75). Anybody who uses silence this way must also be patient to really make it work. After all, how long can you be quiet without wanting to say something to fill the void?

Patience is a hallmark of many of the negotiating tactics you have learned in this book. You are always monitoring yourself to ensure that you are on your highest power level, that you always know where you are in the negotiation, and that you are protecting and preserving the relationship even while you are making the deal. This takes a great deal of self-control—which means it takes a great deal of patience.

There are many ways in which your patience can be tested, putting you at risk for making concessions you shouldn't make, just because you want to reach an agreement. Don't become overly anxious about closing the deal, and don't let the other side see that you are under any time constraints whatsoever. You have to pretend that you have all the time in the world, otherwise they can exercise their power of patience to stonewall you and force you into unwarranted concessions.

Stonewalling can be incredibly frustrating. The negotiator who uses this tactic is counting on wearing down the patience of the other side—and often succeeds.

Thus, it is important to be patient, and not to allow patience to be used against you. Remember that you must never make any concessions under pressure. Instead, try to get the other side to come around and work with you toward a solution. Only then can patience be truly virtuous.

#83: Deal with interruptions creatively

Interruptions can be a very frustrating aspects of any negotiation. When the other side interrupts you, then clearly they are not listening to what you are saying, but are thinking about something else instead, which shows no respect for you or your position. Furthermore, a series of interruptions can defeat the entire negotiation. If one side is not allowed to present their position, and to be heard out, from beginning to end, then a satisfactory agreement will not be reached.

You have two choices to make when you're interrupted. You can either address the question raised by the interruption, or you can ignore it and return to your original conversation. You are at a choice point.

If you chose to return to your point before addressing the content of the interruption, you could pause, smile, and say, "I'll address that in a minute. As I was saying..." and finish your original thought. You might want to make a note of it on your pad of paper, to serve as a reminder. Then, when you're finished with what you're saying, go back to it and respond to the question raised by the interruption. In this way you ensure that you are given enough time to explain your position while also making room for additional issues that pop up during the conversation. This approach will gently but firmly discourage the other side from continuing to interrupt you.

If you decide to abandon your point and address the content of the interruption because you agree that content needs an immediate response, you can move right along with the conversation on the interruption point. This is a valid choice, especially after you have moved beyond the Resistance Stage and are using a joint problem-solving approach.

On your side, you must remember to never, ever interrupt the other party when he or she is speaking. If you're afraid you won't remember what just popped into your head, write it down and bring it up at an appropriate moment. The importance of really listening to the other side cannot be over-emphasized (see #76); you can't arrive at a creative solution without good listening skills. So it is key to remember that a good listener does not interrupt!

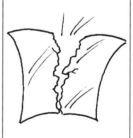

DON'T OBJECT—ASK

One way to keep things from getting hostile is to use questions rather than objections. This keeps the negotiation on a cooperative basis and prevents it from turning into an adversarial situation. Questions should be phrased in a way that helps the other side see reason. For example: "Don't you think that $200 per unit is high when you compare it against the price being offered by XYZ Company?" or "Wouldn't you agree that my throwing in the furniture makes my asking price for the house an absolute bargain?"

#84: Try to prevent hostility before it erupts

When people feel threatened, vulnerable, or exposed, they often become hostile and defensive. This is the last thing you want, because your goal is to arrive at a mutually satisfactory agreement. Therefore it is in everybody's best interest to prevent hostility before it erupts.

To begin, try to remember that you are not out to challenge the beliefs of the other side. You want to create a partnership toward reaching an ideal solution; you don't want to build up an adversarial relationship. Thus, when you disagree with something the other side has said or offered, try phrasing your disagreements as questions or requests for help: "Help me understand your thinking behind your statement that this will successfully work." (instead of "That will never work").

By showing respect for the values and beliefs of the other side, you can usually prevent them from becoming defensive, whereupon you can work together to create a solution. This means never attacking the beliefs of the other side, and keeping everything you say positive and focused on issues. Don't make the disagreements personal. Ask questions, act concerned, and be sure to express your respect and admiration for the other person. It's hard to get hostile with someone who likes you!

Remember that you are out to nurture the relationship, and to create an atmosphere of trust and respect. So you want to do everything you can to avoid making the other side feel threatened or vulnerable. As the song goes—accentuate the positive, and eliminate the negative!

#85: Damage control

Intimidation is a typical bully mind game—the other side may use it to scare you into making concessions or giving in altogether. Typically the other person will get upset and raise his or her voice, then, say, throw a pen or toss up some papers or storm out of the room. This behavior is juvenile and unprofessional, certainly; but it can also achieve its purpose if you let it. You can handle it in the following ways:

1. Keep in mind that you have three choices. You can stay in the room and keep calm; you can stay and match his or her energy level (but *not* the content!); or you can leave.

2. Lower the other sides' expectations by making it clear that you are not susceptible to being bullied. Let them know they can't intimidate you. Don't back down—and don't get scared.

3. Since the negotiation table is no place for unplanned emotions, you can assume that the outburst was planned or at the very least was exaggerated for effect. Therefore, the best approach is to move beyond it. Don't give any credence to the other side's emotions. Simply say something like, "Let's get back to the issues at hand." This lets the other side know that you mean business and won't be intimidated by their outbursts.

#86: Handle personal attacks with equanimity

Sometimes personal attacks on a person's motives or character will enter the negotiation. It may be the result of genuine hostility between two clashing personalities, but more likely it is a tactic used to ruffle your feathers and to knock you off balance. It's best to be prepared for this possibility so that you won't be caught off guard when the other side tries to put you on the defensive by challenging your honesty, ability, or intentions. Here are a few suggestions:

1. Invite criticism. If the other side calls you a liar, ask him or her to elaborate. Find out exactly why he feels you are a liar. Invite her to criticize you more. Taking this tactic catches the other side off guard and makes you seem reasonable, honest, and fair.

2. Let the other side run their course. Just as you would do with a toddler's temper tantrum, let the other person keep ranting until he or she runs out of steam. Wait patiently until they have nothing more to say about you.

3. Insist on objective criteria. If he tells you you're stupid because he thinks so, insist that he give you examples. Say, "I'm really shocked to hear you say that. I need to know exactly

what I did that you think is stupid" or "Exactly what caused you to think that I'm a liar?" By doing this, you force the other side to reason with you.

4. Try not to counterattack. If you let him/her draw you into the fight, all is lost. Try to use the first three tactics above to knock the wind out of his/her sails and return to the negotiation.

5. Keep your self-esteem intact. This is important. Remind yourself that he or she is frustrated by the process, not by you personally. You know you're not stupid or a liar, so don't let the other person's ravings about your character make you feel worthless.

The most important thing to remember when the other side attacks you on a personal level is that they are deliberately trying to get a rise out of you. So your best tactic is: Don't let them! Force him or her to rationalize each of their attacks, and then return the discussion to the issues

#87: Make conflict a productive process

C onflict is another important part of any negotiation. No, I'm not talking about knock-
down, drag-out, screaming brawls. I'm just
talking about emotionally charged situations
which sometimes happen.

During the second Stage of negotiation (Resistance), you may—in fact, you probably will—
encounter disagreement. Don't confuse disagreement with conflict. Two people can definitely disagree without being in conflict. See Secret #77 and
its sidebar for a model on how to reduce the possibility of entering into conflict.

Conflict is an emotionally charged disagreement. It comes from people feeling devalued or
not valued. If, in your negotiation, a conflict comes
to pass, don't look to settle it by discussing facts.
The key to resolving the conflict is to acknowledge
the feelings.

There are several ways you can handle conflict.
You can avoid it. You can compete with it. Or you
can integrate it. This last is the best solution,
because if you work to integrate conflict, you
will end up with a creative, mutually agreeable
solution.

Integrating conflict means that one or both sides
go back and assures the other side that they value

IT'S INEVITABLE

Don't be disturbed or upset if conflict enters the negotiation. Under-stand where it is com-ing from, and make every effort to under-stand the other party with whom you are dealing. Help them understand that, al-though you may dis-agree with their point, you respect and value them as people. Re-member: a disagree-ment is a difference in views or opinions. It can usually be dealt with through discus-sion. A conflict arises only when a person feels either not valued or de-valued. Conflicts have to do with feel-ings first. And then, these feelings get masked by emotionally charged substantive disagreements.

their ideas and point of view, but that they disagree with it. The disagreement can be resolved, the air cleared, and ultimately the other side will feel more appreciated and better understood after the conflict. By doing this, you will have turned con-flict into a productive process in which everybody wins.

WRAPPING IT UP

You're almost home. You've come through a long and arduous negotiation in which you've used some, if not most, of the tools and tactics described in this book. Now you are on the verge of coming to a mutually satisfying agreement. But take care! The final moments of a negotiation can often be the most crucial. Are you really ready to draw the deal to a close? Are you completely sat-isfied with all the agreed upon terms and condi-tions? Is there anything more that needs to be covered in terms of issues and concessions?

The four secrets that follow will help you know just when you are ready to call it a deal.

#88: Use the inward spiral method of achieving closure

The more you apply your Settlement Matrix and other suggestions we have made to the negotiation process, the more you will realize that every negotiation follows an inward spiral process. You start by exploring all the issues—yours and theirs alike. You try to understand the other side's reasons for asking for certain things, and they try to understand your reasons. You say things like, "I heard you ask for an early payment. Would you share with me the thinking behind that request?"

Then you narrow the process by linking the issues. "If I can make the payments earlier, as you requested, then would you be able to lower the price by 15%?" They may counter by linking a different issue, or by just saying, "NO." In this case, you might explore the reason for the "no."

Once you link and trade off issues, you get to a point where an agreement is surfacing. You then move to the last and tighter spiral, the close. You start to make proposals and statements like, "What would you think about doing this?"

Thus, by thinking of the negotiation process as an inward spiral with three rings, you can uncover

BECOME A NEGOTIATION DETECTIVE

Many movies today present fine examples of negotiations. The next time you go to a movie, watch for demands, requests and offers that are negotiated on the big screen. As you watch, look for the inward spiral of closing.

the three distinct movements toward closure: Issue exploration, issue linking, and solution proposal.

#89: Don't agree to a package deal until it's time

One tactic the other side might use in the negotiation is that of presenting a package deal early on in the proceedings. However, in a successful negotiation, you want to discuss each issue, and then arrive at a package deal *at the end*. Such a deal will be achieved through discussion and trading on both sides, and generally is proven to be satisfactory.

When the other side presents a package early on in a negotiation, before any or all of the issues have been discussed individually, it usually means that they want to limit you to an all-or-nothing arrangement, without trading issues. Acceptance of this package will prevent you from getting more on the issues you really care about by giving in on the ones that are less important.

Don't get suckered into accepting a package deal before you're ready! Break up the package and explore each issue independently. If the other side resists your attempt to dissect the package, you may reach an impasse—which is not all that bad at this point in the negotiation. If the other side realizes that they are not going to get an agreement without a little more flexibility on their part, they will either end the negotiation or agree to discuss each issue on its own.

NEVER ON FRIDAY

Settle the deal on Monday, Tuesday, Wednesday, or Thursday, any time you like—but never settle it on Friday, especially in the afternoon. Chances are you've been spending the better part of the week working on this negotiation. By Friday, you're tired. Both your body and your mind will need some rest. Psychologically, this is not the best time to come to a decision. So unless there is a real necessity for settling the deal immediately, don't hesitate to put it off until Monday.

When delaying your decision, you can explain it to the other side in this way: "You know, it's been a long week, and there's a lot to think about. I can't make a decision today. I need the weekend to think about it." There is nothing wrong with being honest, and the other side will respect you for it. It also gives them the same opportunity to think things over and make any necessary changes to the deal. Then, when you return to the table Monday morning, you are both rested and refreshed and able to conclude the deal satisfactorily.

So never agree to a package deal early in the negotiation, as it will only prevent you from getting what you really want. If the other side truly wants to reach an agreement, they will return to the negotiating table with a more flexible attitude; and you can ensure that the package is discussed at the appropriate time—later rather than sooner.

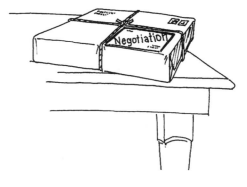

#90: Split the difference only when you're ready

Compromise is a difficult word, and one we generally try to avoid during negotiations. In this book, I have generally used the words "concession" or "trading," which is a kinder, gentler way of describing the process of giving up something in order to get something you want more. But there may come a time when out-and-out compromise is absolutely necessary—that is, both sides must agree to split the difference in order to settle the negotiation, even if the final solution is not the ideal one you were hoping for.

Splitting the difference is a common way to close a deal when all else fails. However, this solution is dangerous when it's used too early. If both sides agree to split the difference because they are anxious or impatient to reach a settlement, then they run the risk of giving up too much too soon. It also is a technique people use when they are not confident negotiators. Generally, it means one side looses more than the other.

You have to be willing to stick it out and put your best effort into the process of trading and making concessions before resorting to compromise. Splitting the difference should be one of your final solution—not your only one.

Here are four things to remember when splitting

the difference:

1. If you ever propose to split the difference, be sure that all other issues that have been discussed are settled and that this split will really close the deal. Use a question such as "Would you be willing to split the difference?" rather than a statement like, "Let's split the difference." The statement is an offer, which can be rejected; whereas the question leaves the matter open-ended.

2. Don't jump to a conclusion prematurely. Make concessions in small steps and with rationales.

3. Remember, patience is the one concession that costs you nothing (see #59). Exercise lots of patience when you are working towards an agreement. Follow the advice given in this book for making concessions, and take turns conceding. How you pace yourself may make all the difference in whether or not you finally have to split the difference.

4. If it's the other side that proposes to split the difference, never accept it immediately. Make a show of how difficult it would be for you to accept the split. In fact, it is sometimes easier to propose a 60-40 split rather than to accept a 50-50 split.

You should never split the difference before you are ready—which means before you have discussed most or all of the issues in your package. It is okay to compromise or meet halfway on an issue if it will close the deal, but only when you know that is what it will take to settle the negotiation. Never allow splitting the difference to take the place of the negotiating!

#91: The last offer is never final

THE EIGHT LAWS OF CLOSING

1. Never fear closing. It is your privilege, your right. It is the way you end a negotiation.

2. Never fear non-acceptance of your suggestion. It is the other side's privilege and right to reject a closing offer.

3. Position and time the closing process for maximum results. Do not try to close a negotiation while there are still open issues on the table or when there are unanswered questions. Close only when then discussion comes to a natural conclusion.

4. Use trial closes when appropriate—that is, test out closing statements to judge how near the other side is to agreeing.

5. When appropriate, position your close to follow summary statements you have made about benefits.

6. If the other side is proposing to close the negotiation, do not interrupt— just listen to their package. You may be able to accept what they are proposing.

7. Use closing statements that appeal to the other side's needs, desires, values, and personality.

8. Plan ahead, and think about how you are going to summarize and close the agreement.

When somebody tells you "this is my final offer," it's usually not. Don't be fooled by this tactic. Respond to it by telling the other person exactly what would be lost if he or she walked away from the deal at this point, and then make a counteroffer. If you do this, the chances are pretty good that they'll be willing to come back to the negotiating table and continue the discussion.

Another way to get around the last-and-final-offer ploy is to accept the offer, but to continue to negotiate. For instance, if I say to you, "I'll give you $200, and that's my final offer," then you could reply, "Okay, let's take that offer and build on it. I'll accept $200 if you agree to move the refrigerator yourself." Don't let the other side force you to close the deal without making a concession.

But, you may be the one using this tactic. If so, it's possible to phrase your last-and-final offer in such a way that it is taken seriously. The more credible the offer, the more likely this tactic is going to work. If you've gone back and forth several times, with each side making concessions, your last offer will be more credible if you tell the other side that your second concession is your final offer. This tactic should be used near the end of the negotiation—but before the offer has dropped below your Least Acceptable Settlement Range.

#92: Make no deal rather than a bad deal

It's okay to leave a negotiation without a deal. Sometimes no matter how hard you try, neither side can reach a satisfactory agreement, therefore there is no agreement. There is certainly no harm in that.

But there is harm in leaving a negotiation with a deal that is bad for one or both parties. Some deals just can't be made. Period. And bad deals can hurt the relationship—sometimes irrevocably. Think about it. If one side is stuck with what they consider to be a bad deal, the relationship will certainly suffer from resentment, and that might put an end to any future negotiations.

Therefore, if given a choice between a very bad deal for one side or the other, or no deal at all, then scrap the deal and save the relationship. This applies to both sides. You shouldn't accept a bad settlement for yourself. Likewise, you should discourage the other side from agreeing to something they might regret later. If you let them go through with it, it may come back to haunt you later in the form of retribution.

Thus, you may reach a point in the negotiation when you realize that it's just not going to work out as a win-win situation, and you are faced with the choice of making a bad deal or no deal at all.

DURING NEGOTIATING CHECKLIST

It helps to keep track of where you are during the negotiation and to know whether you are on track with your plan. This checklist is especially helpful to use between negotiation sessions. To do this, just check the following:

1. My goals:

2. My progress on issues:

3. How I am developing rapport:

4. New information I need to consider:

5. My strategy—is it still appropriate?

6. My tactics—are they working or should I adjust?

7. My timing—present issues now, or delay discussing?

8. My summary of progress made and areas that remain:

9. My willingness to be flexible:

10. My personal confidence level:

11. What Stage of Negotiation we are currently in:

When this happens, always choose the latter. Say, "Gee, I'm really sorry, but I just don't think this is going to work out. Thanks for your time and effort on this deal, and I hope we can get together on something in the future." Always thank the other side for the energy and the effort they expended on the negotiation, and leave the door open for future communication. Never blame the other side for blocking the deal, or take it as a personal affront that the deal won't work. Some deals are better left unmade.

PART III

AFTER YOU NEGOTIATE

FIRST THINGS FIRST

Well, you've done it. The negotiation has drawn to a happy conclusion, and everybody has come out of it smiling. The other side played their cards well and ended up with a winning hand—and better yet, so did you!

But don't run out the door and celebrate just yet. After all, just because you've made a deal that is win-win for all involved doesn't mean the work is over. There are still things to do that will ensure a successful outcome to the negotiation, not just in the immediate future but also down the road. After all, the most important thing that should result from this negotiation is a strong and healthy relationship with the other side.

You can't just agree to a deal and think that's the end of it. You have to follow through on whatever promises you've made and make sure that both sides hold up their ends of the bargain. Failure to do so will violate the trust and mutual respect you worked so hard to build during the negotiation, and that will surely damage both the relationship and any future negotiations, not to mention your reputation. You need to avoid this happening. It's just a matter of taking care of a few major details when all is said and done.

#93: Summarize the agreement

So this is it. All the issues have been resolved, you're getting what you need from the other side, and they're getting what they need from you. But the work isn't quite over yet. You need to summarize what has just taken place, to ensure that the agreement and its terms are fully understood by both sides. You can do this in four easy steps:

Ask the person to take a minute with you to review all the major points of the deal. Check for agreement on each one.

Summarize the entire agreement in a sentence or two. For example, you might say something like, "My understanding of this is that we've agreed to sell you the house for $150,000 and you have agreed to waive the repairs." Ask the other side if they agree with that statement.

If they agree, make it clear that you will leave the negotiation with the understanding that you have a deal. If they don't agree with your summary, now is the time to iron out any problems.

Thank the other side and tell them how much you enjoyed working with them and that you look forward to working with them again.

You did it! Congratulations!

#94: If you have to get approval for the deal

What if you aren't able to make the deal final without first checking with somebody who isn't in the negotiation? This can be tricky, because it can affect how you are perceived by the other side, particularly with regard to the credibility and trust you've built. You don't want to undermine all that by holding up the deal because you have to wait for approval.

To get around the awkwardness of this position, you should first of all make it clear to the other side—right from the start—that you are there to negotiate the agreement, and that you will need to get it approved before it can be ironclad. The best way to do this is to approach it casually. Say something like, "I'm eager to reach agreement on this. Once we've hammered out all the details, I'll just need to run it by my boss. We will have already discussed the issues, so getting her okay shouldn't be a problem, but I do need her signature to make it official."

Go back for a moment to Secret #31, having to do with getting approval beforehand. Now do you see why that was such an important step in the planning process? By going over your plan with your boss before the negotiation begins and getting approval ahead of time, you actually turn this

DON'T BE POWERLESS!

Beginning, middle, or end—no matter where you are in a negotiation, it is important that you do not appear to be powerless. Getting formal approval, in fact, should only apply to the end of the negotiation. Just as you want to deal with the person in power on the other side, so do you not want to appear powerless to them.
So don't run back and check with somebody after you've discussed each issue, otherwise what's the whole point of negotiating internally and getting approval for your plan before you go into the meeting? If the other side views you as powerless to make decisions, they won't want to negotiate with you.

However, it may be the other side that needs approval before finalizing the deal. When this happens, accept it and legitimize it. Say: "I'm so glad you said that, because I need to check with my boss, too."
This lessens any awkwardness that may be caused by the situation.

part of the negotiation process into a pro forma affair. Sure, you still have to get the official okay, but if you've prepared properly and the outcome has met expectations, then getting the boss's signature will be a piece of cake. You will not in fact be holding up finalizing the deal because getting approval will be a quick and easy formality!

So once the deal is arranged, waste no time in getting that approval right away. Don't let the proposal sit on somebody else's desk; why should it sit there when it has already been discussed? The person with the power can and should okay the deal without hesitation or need to review it. Therefore, it is well within reason for you to say, "I need this okayed by the end of the day," and then to follow up to ensure that he or she has signed off on it.

If the person with whom you are negotiating must get approval, you should take the same opportunity. Never leave your deal on the table if they take theirs away. If they return with no changes, you can always say that you also have approval for the agreement the way you both originally designed it. However, if they need a change, then you also will select an issue that you want changed and now, you are both continuing the negotiation.

#95: When the deal is closed, put it in writing

You've negotiated, you've summarized, you've closed the deal, and (if it's necessary) you've gotten approval for the deal. Now you need to put all that hard work into writing. Draft the terms of an agreement. Write down a summary of the package as well as what you agreed to on each separate issue, then send that summary to the other side for their initials.

This important step is something that many people neglect to do after a negotiation. Sometimes they're afraid the other side will be indignant that their word isn't good enough and that taking this step may imply a lack of trust. But this process is more important for remembering what you agreed to than for making sure that everybody sticks to the agreement. This is something that can be emphasized when presenting it to the other side. Just tell them that you want to make sure everybody has the same understanding and record of the agreement. In this way you will reassure them that it's not a matter of trust, but purely a matter of record-keeping.

CLEAN-UP WORK

You've spent a lot of time preparing a large meal, and to your delight everybody has walked away from the table satisfied, if not downright contented—including yourself. But there is still a pile of dishes in the sink that needs washing. And that's a chore that shouldn't be put off.

Clean-up work is just another part of the process; but it shouldn't be too difficult. The important thing is that you take care of it sooner rather than later. It's a simple matter of follow-up—of living up to your promises and of summarizing your experiences for the benefit of future negotiations.

#96: It doesn't end with a handshake

T he point of this secret cannot be stressed enough: *Just because the meeting is over, that doesn't mean your work is done.* There is still plenty to do, and it involves living up to the obligations you made during the negotiation.

Keep in mind all that we've talked about in terms of building trust and preserving the relationship. You also need to be concerned about your reputation. Remember: People do business with people they like and trust. And they don't like and trust people who do not keep their word and fail to hold up their end of the bargain.

What does this mean? It means you have to *deliver on what you promised.* Even if you're not the one who is directly responsible for shipping the goods or for paying the bill or for physically completing the transaction, you still have to ensure that everything you said would happen from your end *does* happen, and that the other side is satisfied with the results. If you say, "Those materials will be delivered by a week from Friday," only to have your shipping department mistakenly schedule the delivery two weeks later, how does that make you look? If your side consistently fails to make good on promises in a negotiation, then, in time, you will find yourself negotiation-less. Nobody will want to deal with you, because you will have developed a reputation for failure to deliver.

You can't just shake hands with somebody and then walk out of the room thinking your part of the deal is done. It doesn't work that way. You have a responsibility to follow up and ensure that promises that have been made are happening according to the plan and schedule. Sometimes that means you have to negotiate internally with people who will deliver on your agreement; or perhaps you will have to remind someone internally to send something or to follow-up on something you've delegated. Do whatever you have to do in order to ensure that your part of the agreement is being kept. By doing so, you cement your reputation for trustworthiness—and ensure that future negotiations are welcomed.

#97: Make notes for your files— and yourself

We've already learned how important it is to take notes during the negotiation (see #46). And yes, taking notes can be a drag. Yet, it is important that you remember what was resolved and how each issue was approached by the other side. If you have notes to refer to, then you'll be better prepared for your next negotiation with that party.

Thus, in addition to the notes you take during the course of the negotiation, you should also jot down a few notes afterward in a notebook you keep exclusively for this purpose. In the main, you might answer these quick questions for each negotiation you encounter:

1. Who was present at the negotiation?

2. What issues seemed important to the other side?

3. What issues were decided upon?

4. What issues still need to be resolved (if any)?

5. What about the negotiation was significant, that might come in useful for future negotiations?

Notes like these are especially useful if you've left the negotiation without a deal and will have to resume the talks sometime later. But more importantly, they help to clarify your understanding of what took place in the meeting(s) and leave you better prepared for future negotiations.

AFTER EFFECTS

Finally you reach the point when you can relax. Your work is well and truly done. You have succeeded in concluding a win-win negotiation with superb skill, and have every reason to pat yourself on the back! Even if the outcome wasn't exactly what you wanted, you should still feel proud of yourself because you did a good job, and you protected the relationship with the other side.

There will be after effects, of course, especially if it was a particularly grueling negotiation. Sometimes you may be giddy with your success. Other times you may feel crushed by your failure. Indeed, the clean-up work may not apply just to the negotiation but also to yourself. Here are just a few tips for expert handling of whatever may follow the closing of a deal.

#98: Taking stock of how you did

It's time for a little self-evaluation. After each negotiation that you complete, take a few minutes to answer these easy questions, in order to determine how good you were and how you can do better the next time. Negotiating is an ongoing learning process, and you'll see yourself improve with each deal you make. These questions provide an easy way to track your own progress:

1. Were your goals appropriate?

2. Was your planning on target?

3. Should you have spent more time in the planning process? Where?

4. How well did the Matrix work?

5. What important points do you want to remember for next time?

6. If you could do it over, what would you do again?

You will be able to identify techniques and methods you should continue to use because they are successful for you. You will also be able to identify patterns of weaknesses that you will want to work on in order to improve. Examining yourself in this way will surely help you become a better negotiator. It just takes practice!

ARE YOU IMPROVING?

We suggest that you start a "Negotiation Notebook" in which you take one page per negotiation and jot down some notes and evaluations for yourself. After you keep the book for a time, you will notice repeated patterns. Here are some items you should include:

✓ *What contributed to the success of the negotiation?*

✓ *What were your weaknesses in the negotiation process?*

✓ *What lessons did you learn?*

✓ *What should you remember to do or not to do next time?*

✓ *What should you remind yourself of next time?*

✓ *If you had to do the negotiation over again, what would you do differently?*

Look for patterns of behavior that contributed to your success so you can repeat them. Also look for patterns of behavior that create weaknesses in your style. These are areas you need to improve.

#99: Not Getting the deal does not mean you failed

It is always important to remember that any ne-gotiation that preserves the relationship between two sides, no matter what its outcome, is a suc-cessful negotiation. Perhaps things didn't work out the way you had hoped. The big order you had promised your boss didn't materialize due to a fail-ure to come to agreement on terms. The purchase of a new fleet of company cars fell through be-cause the other side wouldn't budge on the price. The boat you tried to hire to take your family fish-ing wasn't available for the time you wanted it. Any number of things can happen that can prevent the negotiation from resulting in a deal. You have to accept that this happens sometimes, and then move on.

Sometimes, not being able to culminate an agreement can be very disappointing. Yet even when things don't work out the way we had hoped, we are always able to draw something from our experiences that strengthen us and make us better prepared for "the next time." Think of what you have learned from this negotiation and use it to your advantage in the next one. Even our dis-appointments have something to teach us; keep that in mind as you grapple with a collapsed deal. Take stock of yourself (see #98) and ask yourself what you can use from this negotiation that will help you in the future. In time, you will see that our successes are often rooted in our failures.

Most important is how well you protected and preserved your relationship with the other side, for that is the true measure of your success. If, at the end, they walk away from the table with admiration and respect for you and your position, and with confidence in your honesty and integrity, then you have truly succeeded, no matter whether the deal was closed or not. The sky may be a little gray today, but the sun will still come out tomorrow, because you have done the right thing and have every reason to be proud of yourself. So give yourself a pat on the back, no matter what—you deserve it!

#100: The snowball effects of negotiation

One of the greatest benefits that comes from applying honesty and integrity in your negotiating skills is that it not only ensures a continued good relationship with the current party, it also enhances your reputation with other parties with whom you might end up negotiating. In fact, with each negotiation, you are building up your reputation, for the other side is sure to pass on the word about you—and word spreads quickly. If you were deceptive and underhanded in your dealings, then others will know it soon enough and you'll find most people will not want to deal with you. But, if you establish and maintain a reputation for fairness and being a straight dealer, they will be battering down your door to do business with you.

Like a mound of snow rolling down a hill, your reputation as a negotiator builds with each deal you close—and even the ones you don't close. It's how people perceive you that counts, and that contributes to this snowball effect. It's important to remember this. Often we look at a negotiation as a one time deal—that is, we get what we want and then we get out. But as you have learned by now, that's not all there is to a negotiation. If you are dealing with somebody with whom you have an ongoing business or personal relationship, then each negotiation will naturally affect the next.

So keep this in mind if you decide to try to manipulate or outwit the other side, or if you make a deal that's bad for them. They are sure to remember it in your next negotiation, and it is just as sure to work against you as a result. The relationship counts. Treat it with honesty and respect so that the snowball effect works for you, not against you.

**BECOME A
HIGH-PERFORMANCE
NEGOTIATOR**

*You have the secrets
now. All you need is
the practice.*

*1. Look for every op-
portunity to negotiate
(even if you only pre-
pare the negotiation
mentally)—in restau-
rants, in stores, as you
watch sitcoms on TV.
The more aware you
become that everything
can be negotiated, the
more your confidence
will build.*

*2. Plan, plan, plan.
Never enter any type
of a negotiation (no
matter how insignifi-
cant) without creating
a Matrix. Not only is
the practice helpful,
but you will begin to
identify many more
issues that can be
brought up. Addition-
ally, it clarifies your
thinking about the
results your seeking.*

Continued ➡

#101: Be a winner with class

How do you want to feel at the end of a nego-tiation? Like a winner, right? Well, the other side does, too, and part of your job was to ensure that they felt that way.

A good part of protecting the relationship in-cludes the way you handle yourself after all is said and done. This means you don't crow, "Ha, ha, I won!" and you don't do a victory dance, either. What you should do is express your pleasure at the arrangement you've worked out, and you thank the other side for their contribution. Mention one or two specific contributions—i.e., "Your idea about reducing the price in favor of changing the due date really helped clinch the deal." By doing this, you reassure the other side that their negotiation, too, was successful.

It also helps to reiterate the benefits of the deal to both sides, which serves as a reminder of how important this negotiation was to both of you. Put it in the context of your relationship. For example, you could say something like: "I'm glad we could make this deal. Since we were able to agree on these issues, it paves the way for future deals of this kind." Such a statement reinforces your faith in the relationship.

Remember: Negotiating is all about relation-ships, and relationships are all about making the other side feel good about themselves. People must not only win, they must feel like winners—and you can make that happen.

It's this simple: The most successful negotiations are those in which *both* sides are winners!

———

3. Flexibility is the name of the game. Appear to be willing to work with the other person to develop a workable agreement for both of you and you will improve the success ratio of your negotiation encounters.

4. Remember that each negotiator has personal needs—the need to be respected, valued, appreciated, the need to be taken seriously, to name a few. Treat each person you negotiate with the way you would like to be treated.

5. Don't forget to approach and to match each person's social style. The more you can keep a person in his or her comfort zone, the more you will be able to establish a rapport and a relationship with him or her. Remember: people do business with people they like and trust. Who do you like and trust? Right, people who are like you and share your values. It's easier to negotiate with people who you like and respect.

AUTHOR'S NOTE:

We have covered many concepts and presented many ideas in this book. Now it's up to you to apply the secrets and to practice. Don't expect mastery in one reading. Use this book as a resource which you refer to from time to time. You will find that sometimes, when you pick up the book and read something - even something you've read before - you read it differently and it means something else. That is because you are growing and expanding your understanding of the negotiation process. As you journey through your negotiations, you will become more comfortable and more skilled. If I have positively contributed in any way to your journey, I thank you for the opportunity.